Above and Beyond

Above and Beyond

Tim Mack, the Pole Vault, and the Quest for Olympic Gold

Bill Livingston

The Kent State University Press
Kent, Ohio

© 2008 by The Kent State University Press, Kent, Ohio 44242
All rights reserved
Library of Congress Catalog Card Number 2008014203

ISBN 978-0-87338-974-7

Manufactured in the United States of America

Library of Congress Cataloging-in-Publication Data
Livingston, Bill.
    Above and beyond : Tim Mack, the pole vault, and the quest for Olympic
gold / by Bill Livingston.
        p. cm.
    ISBN 978-0-87338-974-7 (hardcover : alk. paper) ∞
1. Mack, Tim, 1972–   2. Track and field athletes—United States—Biography.
3. Vaulting. I. Title.
    GV697.M24L58 2008
    796.42092—dc22
    [B]
                                                            2008014203

British Library Cataloging-in-Publication data are available.

12 11 10 09 08   5 4 3 2 1

This book is for my children, Sondra, Julianne,
and Billy, who all reached high bars, and for my wife
Marilyn, who always knew I could do it.

Contents

Preface

Harrison Dillard

Having spent some 25 years as a track athlete and the next 52 as a fan, follower and sometimes official, I think it's safe to say I've been around the sport in some capacity all my life. I've known success and occasional failure.

I've formed opinions about the events and the competitors, just as I am sure most people have.

The athletes I have wondered about most are distance runners and pole-vaulters. The punishment endured by those in these two persuasions would seem to me to be tantamount to torture. The worst of it is that it is self-inflicted for the most part. Rest assured that while I may think of them as being just a smidgen strange to take up such pursuits, my respect and admiration for them has no limits.

That brings me to the subject of Timothy Mack, who added his name to the list of Cleveland-area athletes who have won gold in what many consider the greatest sports spectacle in the world, the Olympic Games.

Tim's career for the most part has been no different from those of thousands of others with dreams of reaching the ultimate level. I too have shared that dream. Much like Tim, it was essentially, as the saying goes, "just for the love of the game." It was a means of self-expression. It was a desire to do something better than anybody else on earth.

There was a price to pay in physical, mental, and emotional terms. There would be little in the way of material or financial gain.

I guess it boils down to how and by what standards you measure success. Read on to see how Tim Mack did it and to learn something about pole vaulting and some of its most storied characters.

A member of the USA Track and Field Hall of Fame, Dillard won the 100 meters at the 1948 Olympics after not qualifying in his specialty, the 110-meter high hurdles. He came back and won the gold medal in that event in the 1952 Olympics, becoming the only man to turn a double in that event. Dillard attended Cleveland's East Tech, the same high school as Jesse Owens. The best hurdler in the world after World War II, in which he served, Dillard was inspired to become an Olympian when Owens, riding in a car in a victory parade after the 1936 Olympics, winked at Dillard and said hello.

Acknowledgments

No book (much less one about the pole vault) is the result of one person's labor.

I would like to thank *Plain Dealer* (PD) colleague Tom Feran, without whom there would be no *Above and Beyond*. He was the book's first editor and was a never-ending source of encouragement.

PD colleague Mark Dawidziak steered me through the byways of the book world, and I cannot thank him enough.

I was a poor outliner as a boy, and the PD's Mary Schmitt Boyer helped with that, and with encouragement, and with the edifying example of her own books.

Elton Alexander, my PD buddy at many a Kent State or University of Akron basketball game over the years, was always interested and always ready to listen.

Dr. Henry Briggs contributed the title to chapter 6 and encouragement as a true Woodrow Wilson News reporter.

The late John Kotowich, a University of Akron pole-vaulter back in the day, showed me that the bar is never too high. He was a great friend and a fine gentleman. I miss him.

The great Texas columnist Blackie Sherrod, who could not write a note for the milkman without it being a small gem, encouraged me and wrote a fine essay about pole vaulting in the bamboo and sawdust days that gave me an appreciation for that era.

Tom Surber of USA Track and Field provided phone numbers.

My wife, Marilyn, suggested the title. My daughter, Sondra, typed many pages flawlessly. My friend, Leo Spagnola, reminded me it was a labor of love.

Former *Dallas Morning News* colleague John Anders and his wife Helen gave the book an enthusiastic early thumbs-up, which provided a lot of early momentum.

Clevelander Bob Ramsak of Trackprofile.com helped me with details of injuries suffered by top pole-vaulters.

PD sports editor Roy Hewitt gave the book his blessing.

Former PD colleague Dick Zunt was an invaluable resource when it came to St. Ignatius High School, his alma mater.

My mentor from Kenosha, Wisconsin, John McEvoy, gave me another great example of how to do this writing stuff with his mysteries.

My other mentor, the retired Bill Millsaps, former editor of the *Richmond Times-Dispatch,* has listened to many a rant over many a glass of brown in his day. I tried to do justice to pole vaulting the way he honored the integrity of newspapering.

Jud Logan, hammer thrower supreme, was also an early advocate of the book. Tim Mack's agent, Chris Layne, approved the project early on and always sought to help. My agent, Lois de la Haba, pumped me up when I was down.

The wonderful men and women of the pole vault community could not have been more generous with their time. Jim Bemiller ("B") was especially selfless, reading the manuscript for technical mistakes. Any that remain are my fault, not his.

In addition to "B," I would like to thank Don Bragg, the great Sergey Bubka, Steve Chappelle, Stacy Dragila, Ed and Terri Dare, Bob Fraley, Greg Hull, Jan Johnson, Russ Johnson, Brian Kelly, Chuck Kyle, Brian Mondschein, Tim O'Hare, Bob Richards, Rob Sachs, Ralph Schreiber, Bob Seagren, Toby Stevenson, Jenn Stuczynski, Stanley Underwood, Grace Upshaw, Joe Whitney, and Don and Arlene Mack. Not to mention Tim, who cleared barriers at least 7 meters high.

Those Magnificent Men and Their Flying Schemes

Track and field represents the genesis of competition. Mankind has wondered who was faster or stronger as long ago as the funeral games in the *Iliad,* and despite the taint of drug abuse, track and field today remains the purest sport conceptually. It symbolizes the highest plane of endeavor, because it can quantify human limits more than any other sport.

The ancient Olympics eventually included chariot racing, discus throwing, boxing, and wrestling, but the first Olympic sport was a run the length of a field that amounted to nearly 200 meters.

Like the pole vault, the marathon wasn't part of the ancient Olympics. The longest race then was only 4,614 meters, or about 2.9 miles. The marathon commemorated the probably legendary professional runner Phidippides, who raced 26 miles from the coastal plain to Athens to announce the victory of the Greeks over the Persians at the Battle of Marathon. Sadly, after his announcement, Phidippides fell dead, electrolyte-rich sports drinks not having been invented yet.

The pole vault developed later and farther north. It took the skirmishes to the sky, so the gods lounging on Mount Olympus could enjoy them. Although the Celts and Cretans used poles in jumping competitions, the latter to clear charging bulls, the sport's modern roots were in the Netherlands. Dutch farmers used poles to vault across drainage ditches in a land in which every foot of soil is below sea level. Jumping poles were also used in marshy parts of England. The Germans added pole-jumping to gymnastics exercises in the 1850s. Later, the Ulverston Cricket Club of Lancashire, England, was credited with changing it to a vertical competition.

Originally, an iron stake was embedded in the end of a solid ash, spruce, or hickory pole. Pole-vaulters climbed the pole, which they drove stake-first into the ground, then toppled over the crossbar in a sitting position. It was more elegant than falling off a very tall three-legged stool, but not by much.

In 1889 Americans banned moving the hands along the pole to climb it. Lightweight bamboo poles arrived around 1900. Bamboo, botanically speaking, is actually a giant grass. The woody, cane-like stem, which was much lighter than solid poles, was used for vaulting poles. The vault box to receive the pole came soon after. The acrobatic upside-down position, clearing the crossbar feet first with the abdomen down, became the most efficient method of clearance.

By 1936 the material for poles was no longer officially restricted to wood or bamboo. Metal poles became the implements of choice in the 1950s. They were safer than bamboo, which could snap as if it were feeding time at the panda exhibit in the zoo. Some elite pole-vaulters used aluminum, but more used what was known as "Swedish steel." Swedish iron ore was free of phosphorus, which could contaminate the steel-making process. It was a high-quality steel that was heavier than aluminum and had minimal flex properties (although a fast jumper could coax a few reluctant inches of bend out of it). There were also alloy poles, such as Duralium, a brand name that consisted of aluminum, copper, magnesium, manganese, and silicon.

The heaviest metal poles were so inflexible and hard to hold that Ron Morris, the 1960 Olympic silver medalist, would heat the tape on the grip with a can of Sterno and matches. This "cooking" of the pole allowed it to stick to his hands. Metal poles, often generically called "steel" poles, put a premium on brute strength because they were so rigid.

The modern era began with the more flexible fiberglass pole in the late 1950s and 1960s. Herb Jenks, an engineer with the Browning Arms Company, developed an alternative to steel poles while working with fiberglass tubes to be used in the manufacture of bows and arrows. The fiberglass pole is essentially a hollow tube composed of filaments of glass embedded in a matrix of polymer resin. The fiberglass pole was far lighter than any of the previous implements, allowing pole-vaulters to run faster. Fiberglass poles now weigh between three and six pounds, although, because they are carried near one end, their "leveraged weight" is substantially more. Experiments have shown that elite pole-vaulters are lugging over thirty-seven pounds in "carry weight" by the time they reach takeoff.

Today's poles are made of layers of carbon fiber or graphite and fiberglass composite materials. They bend like a backslider's willpower. And yet a modern pole, seemingly so thin and fragile, can stop a 175-pound man running in excess of 20 mph and then help propel him over a bar close to 20 feet above the ground. It isn't really a very long magic wand, but it is close.

In fact, fiberglass was considered so flimsy an implement for such daring that Jenks became a minor celebrity in his own right. As pole-vaulters began to use the new implement, Jenks modified its stiffness and tapered the grip. The whippier pole caused records to go almost literally out of sight.

Between 1960, the last time a vaulter won an Olympic medal on a metal pole, and 1964, after fiberglass had been widely used, the Olympic record improved from Don Bragg's 15–5 (4.70 meters) to Fred Hansen's 16–8¾ (5.10), a quantum leap of 7.8 percent. To put this in perspective, consider that when Bob Beamon became the first man to long-jump 29 feet (no one else had even jumped 28) at the 1968 Olympics, the seemingly astonishing improvement in the world record came to only 6.3 percent.

Pole-vaulters often name their poles, much as Roy Hobbs dubbed his miracle bat "Wonderboy" in *The Natural.* An online survey of pole nicknames turned up "Bad Boy," "Pimpin' Pole," "Black Death," "El Jefe Negro" (The Black Chief), and the generic "Pole," to whom urgent pleas were addressed, as in: "Okay, Pole. Nice Pole. C'mon, Pole. Time to flick my fat ass over that bar." A former pole-vaulter at Purdue noted that Boilermakers who ran through the pit too often in practice had to vault on a pole with permanent black ink letters spelling out "P-U-S-S-Y."

Sand was replaced by sawdust in the landing area and then by landing mattresses. The pole-vaulter tries to land on his back on the mattresses. In the old days, many landings were crashes. The advent of the fiberglass pole in the 1960s made for happier landings—a necessary step for the sport to progress to greater heights. Foam-rubber pads had replaced sawdust in most meets by the decade's end. Pole-vaulters tried to land on their feet in the sand pit era with their knees bent, followed, at worst, by a gentle rump bump into the sand. But the contortionist's demands of writhing over the bar in any possible manner caused pole-vaulters to make landings on their shoulders, back or even belly. The sand in the pit was mixed with sawdust to keep it from packing together, but landing in the stuff was no day at the beach. *Life* magazine ran a memorable two-page photo spread of John Pennel's first 17-foot jump in 1963. In it, Pennel is captured landing on his back in less sawdust than a sapling could have produced.

The pole vault skews to the extremes of human behavior. Pole-vaulters must have the same double helix of DNA as fighter pilots and daring young men on the flying trapeze. Astronaut Edwin "Buzz" Aldrin was once a pole-vaulter. The second man to walk on the surface of the moon, Aldrin was jumping into great adventures on the end of a pole as a teenager in Montclair, New Jersey, years before the *Eagle* landed.

The pole vault tends to draw physically imposing, steely-eyed types, capable of crashing a *People* magazine "Most Beautiful People" list. Other male celebrities who were pole-vaulters included Robert Culp, who was second in the state of California in high school; Shannon Hoon, the late lead singer of Blind Melon; and the undeniably hunky Patrick Swayze, who starred in the popular movies *Ghost* and *Dirty Dancing*. In addition, rock singer-songwriter John Mellencamp was a 12–6 jumper in high school. Morice Fredrick "Tex" Winter, one of the innovattors of basketball's triangle offense, pole-vaulted at Compton (California) Junior College and Southern Cal, clearing 14–4 for the Trojans.

Every pole-vaulter must overcome the sensible objection that such upside-down calisthenics are a deep affront to his sense of self-preservation. A pupil once said to 1972 Olympic bronze medalist Jan Johnson that pushing off the pole while upside down was "not human nature." Snapped Johnson: "It's also not human nature to get a fiberglass pole, run balls out, and plant the pole. Now get out there and try again!"

Poles are calibrated for the pole-vaulter's weight. Vaulters are seldom heavier than 190–195 pounds, because more weight means more payload to lift. The poles also vary in stiffness as determined by their "flex rating." This is determined by putting a fifty-pound weight on the middle of a pole with end supports and measuring how much is displaced. The poles of Sergey Bubka, the Ukrainian considered by many to be the best pole-vaulter ever, were stiffer than a slug of white lightnin' from a Mason jar.

The rules used to state that if a pole passed under the crossbar after a pole-vaulter released it, the vault constituted a miss. That rule hasn't applied in many years. It is considered a miss, however, if the pole-vaulter moves his lower hand above the upper or moves his upper hand. This is considered "climbing" the pole. If a pole breaks, the vaulter gets another attempt.

The pegs that hold the crossbar were shortened in 2003 from 3 inches to 2¼ (75 millimeters to 55), putting a premium on clean clearances, free of the jiggling and quivering of bars brushed by the pole-vaulters. It is a big reduction, amounting to 25 percent of the previous length. Imagine what havoc might be created in the relays if the baton were sawed off in the same way.

The crossbar is fiberglass, but on either end are rubber tips which sit on the pegs. At the same time as the pegs were whittled down, the tips were changed from a square configuration to one that is flat on one side and curved on the other. The theory is that if the bar is struck hard enough to bounce or roll, it will become dislodged and not come back to rest on a square side.

American coaches wondered if Bubka supported the rules change in order to protect his records. The rumor began as Bubka rose in power in international track and field after his retirement. The coaches wondered why the worldwide governing body for track and field, the International Association of Athletics Federations (IAAF), didn't test the shorter pegs more thoroughly. This change to the sport, after all, is similar to raising the mound and moving the fences back in baseball. Shortening the pegs and making the end of the bar liable to be dislodged by a clatter of butterfly wings is hardly fan-friendly in a difficult, crowd-pleasing event. As was argued on track and field Internet message boards at the time, the changes in equipment specifications amount to cases of disadvantaging later athletes. "What's next?" one wonders. "Electrifying the bar?"

In fact, some coaches believe it is impossible to compare post-2003 performances with those that went before it with more forgiving pegs. Many track and field fans speak of the years after 2003 as the beginning of the "clean clearance" era.

The pole vault was one of the last events in track and field to yield to gender equity. Because of its danger and difficulty, it was an Olympic sport for men only until the Sydney Games in 2000. The arrival of women with their skimpy costumes and record-setting binges brought a whole new set of fans to the sport.

USA Today rated pole-vaulting over 15 feet as the third-hardest feat in sports, behind hitting a major league pitch and driving a racecar 200 mph. It is as perilous as it is difficult. On a per capita basis, pole-vaulting is responsible for more fatal and "catastrophic" injuries (defined as injuries causing paralysis) than football. Poles can snap when they are too light for a pole-vaulter's weight and overbend. The greatest danger is missed landings, however. When they jump, pole-vaulters take both the pole and their own lives in their hands. Few vaulters at the world-class level wear protective helmets, although head injuries are obviously massive when suffered after falling from the equivalent of a second-story window and missing the foam-rubber landing pads. From 18 feet, a vaulter weighing 175 pounds falls at a rate of 24 mph. Such a mass screaming down towards the pit at 35.2 feet per second packs a wallop of 6,160 pounds. Of course, the actual effect must be modified; penetrating deeply into a soft mattress reduces the force significantly.

The modern pole vault is track and field's most spectacular event. It begins with a sprint down a runway that is 45 meters long (49 yards, 18 inches). As in most of the other straightaway events—the 100 meters, 100 and 110 hurdles, long jump, and triple jump—a tailwind is beneficial in the pole vault. If there is a headwind, the pole-vaulter will cover less ground with each stride. To counteract this, the pole-vaulter moves back at the start. If there is a tailwind, he or she moves forward. Tim Mack, the 2004 Olympic men's pole vault gold medalist, begins his run at between 133–135 feet (40.5–41 meters), depending on conditions.

Elite pole-vaulters use an approach (or run towards the pole vault pit) that amounts to between eighteen and twenty strides. If the runner is 1 inch off on each stride, he will miss his optimum launch window by almost 2 feet. That is why the marks used to check the course of the approach are so critical.

The biggest factor in determining a successful vault is not improved equipment. The jump's potential depends most critically on the speed the pole-vaulter reaches before takeoff and his or her height. Velocity also directly relates to the size of pole that the vaulter can bend, which translates to height. On his biggest jump of 20–2, the 6-foot Bubka was timed at 9.94 meters per second in the final five meters before launch, or 22.3 mph. The pole vault requires precise footwork on the runway, explosiveness on the takeoff, coordination on the pole, agility in getting off it, and the right stuff to even attempt the thing. It requires an all-out sprint while burdened with a cumbersome implement and exemplifying posture a runway model would envy. Other than that, anyone can do it.

While world-class 100-meter men reach 25–26 mph, they aren't carrying long poles. Sprinters lean forward to increase velocity, but pole-vaulters must run with an upright torso to increase their chances of success in the next phase of the jump.

Long arms increase the takeoff angle off the ground because the pole is higher and there is less distance to vertical at liftoff. Powerful hands are assets too. Although critical exceptions can be found, such as American Olympian Scott Huffman and 2005 World Champion Rens Blom of the Netherlands, the shortest distance from the earth to the stars in pole-vaulting is usually a tall guy with long arms, big hands and a stout heart.

The takeoff point varies depending on how high the pole-vaulter grips on the pole and how tall he or she is. Most elite vaulters use 5.10-meter poles (16 feet, 8¾ inches), although a few use 5.20 (17–0½). Tim Mack, the 2004 Olympic gold medalist, was on 16–8¾ poles in 2004. They take off between 12 feet, 6 inches and 14 feet from the vaulting box. Mack optimally launches at 13–6, but he can jump effectively anywhere from 12–9 to 13–6. Biomechanically, the optimum is to have the vaulter's takeoff foot directly beneath the extended top hand on the pole.

After the pole-vaulter "plants" (jams) the pole into the vaulting box, he jumps off the ground, bending the pole with his weight. The kinetic energy from the run is then transferred to the pole. It is stored as potential energy in the form of a compressed spring. As it straightens from a 150-degree arc, the pole returns the energy to the pole-vaulter. Modern poles are constructed of such advanced materials that they waste very little energy when they bend, and they have a good ratio of strength-to-weight. The effect of all this is similar to that of a catapult operated by a man with an itchy trigger finger.

Field events, the "throws" and "jumps," are so dependent on difficult-to-master techniques that they require a bigger complement of athletic skills than track. For example, a pole-vaulter is both a sprinter and a gymnast. A triple jumper must have speed, spring, and the resilience to rebound from the shock of landing to jump again. The sprints demand a spare, efficient style free of wasted motion, attention to stride pattern and other concerns. But basically, a sprint is no more complicated than putting one foot in front of the other and sometimes turning left.

Since the pole vault is considered one of the four "jumps," along with the high jump, triple jump and long jump, pole-vaulters usually speak in terms of jumps, not vaults. The pole vault probably gets more attention than all the other field events combined due to its spectacular nature.

An elite pole-vaulter knows endurance is a premium virtue. The bar is elevated after multiple clearances by only 5 centimeters, or about 2 inches. The pole-vaulter competes against the clouds and the clock. If more than three competitors are still alive, he has one minute to jump; for two or three he has two minutes; and, if jumping alone and presumably for a meet or a world record, five minutes. Ties are broken by fewer misses or by a jump-off at the last bar successfully cleared.

Like the high jump, the pole vault offers nearly countless chances for a competitor to take the lead. Clear a new height on any of three tries, raise the bar, up the stakes, push yourself and your competitors to new levels, and climb forever toward the golden glow at the end of the pole.

"Citius, altius, fortius," reads the Olympic motto in Latin. Faster, higher, stronger. Higher is a pole-vaulter's particular creed. A pole-vaulter jumps higher by a magnitude of two and a half times than a high jumper. A world-class male pole-vaulter goes almost twice as high as a basketball rim. A pole-vaulter goes over the rim, the 11½-foot high white square on the backboard, the backboard itself, the 24-second shot clock bolted to its top, and damn near the rafters and catwalks high above.

Actually, of course, pole-vaulters do not reach the sky in any meaningful sense. But the extremity of altitude, attained without the use of ropes, pitons, sherpa guides, and a handy mountainside, forms the way pole-vaulters are seen both within the fraternity of flight and without. Viewed from the ground, the crossbar seems to be a thin line drawn across the sky, marking the border of possibility. Most of us rooted to the common clay would never dare the air. Not pole-vaulters. They have no patience with grays and neutral colors. They take the imagination higher. They are dreamers without borders.

1 · Dark Horse

No one wants to be like Sergey. Not in the United States, not in a sports culture dominated by ESPN *SportsCenter* highlights and instant gratification. Besides, there is no playground culture to pole-vaulting, the sport Ukrainian Sergey Bubka mastered the way an angel does clouds.

But Tim Mack was a pole-vaulter, and thus, throughout his adolescence and adulthood, he was different. Even among pole-vaulters, who usually belong to the fraternity of daredevils and a society of swagger, he stood apart. More cerebral than visceral, a sort of thinking man's stunt man, he thought himself over the bar as much as he led a banzai charge on it. Like every pole-vaulter of his generation, he looked up to Bubka in the same way that every basketball player who wanted to be like Mike looked up to Michael Jordan. A poster of the Ukrainian legend hung on Mack's bedroom wall throughout high school and college.

On the last day of September in the Olympic year of 2004, Mack parked his black Mitsubishi Montero, with the Cleveland Browns license plate, in the tiny faculty parking lot at St. Ignatius High School, located only a mile or so from downtown Cleveland. It was easy to spot his SUV, because a willowy white fiberglass vaulting pole was lashed to the baggage rack on the roof.

To appreciate where Mack was then in the high, golden sun of a perfect autumn morning, you had to know where he had been. He was, in a sport in which men try to reach unreachable bars, the impossible dream come true. If you knew the story, the pole could have been a lance and the truck Rocinante, Don Quixote's horse.

It was "Tim Mack Day" at his alma mater, as the Jesuit all-boys school honored the Athens Olympics pole vault gold medalist with a lunch and a rally. At lunch, Mack's mother, Arlene, after a sneaky shopping trip to Great Northern Mall near their house in suburban Westlake, presented Tim with a secret weapon: a Superman T-shirt. There were times in his life when, both knowingly and unknowingly, he had done impressions of a comic book superhero—tying a towel around his neck to trail behind him on a dive into the waters of an abandoned rock quarry as part of a hazing ritual or taking his victory lap in Athens while holding an American flag that streamed behind him like the stars and stripes forever. But Mack knew the truth behind the joke. Super powers were not the reason he had won. He had dug the secrets of the pole vault out of the steel "box," the launching pad where the pole slammed down; he had rooted in the ground of his coach's yard for them; he had tinkered with makeshift contraptions of his own devising to correct his posture and increase his strength; in a notebook, he had entered everything he skimmed off the occasional glories of success or gleaned from the mounting rubble of failure.

"Thanks, Mom. This won't get any attention," Mack said, examining the T-shirt with the block "S" on it.

As the teenagers ate, Mack shuffled from table to table and visited with them. Everyone wanted a glimpse of the gold medal. The students goggled at it as they asked for his autograph on their T-shirts, book bags, laptop computers, and Gatorade bottles. The teachers also approached the medal with a sense of wonder. A Greek teacher photocopied both sides of the medal in order to translate the medal's Greek inscription that was taken from a victory ode the poet Pindar composed when the ancient Olympics were held in Olympia.

"Is it legal to Xerox a gold medal?" asked Mack's old coach, Chuck "Chico" Kyle.

"The first thing I thought of when I won is that I did not want this to change me as a person," Mack said, as the photocopier whirred and flashed. "The gold medal is something bigger than I am. I always had an image of what gold medal winners were like. You know, people like Jesse Owens. That I am actually one of them is surreal."

The most recognizable athletic bauble in the world, an Olympic gold medal isn't really gold; it's sterling silver that has been gilded with at least six grams of gold (about one-fifth of an ounce). Of course, it isn't the metal that makes it so valuable, but the mettle it took to win it. That day in Cleveland, it seemed as if no woman who had ever accepted a ring from a beau on bended knee had to show off her hardware as often as Mack did.

If the gold wasn't enough to impress the students and faculty at St. Ignatius High School, the uprights were. Not content to leave Mack's feat to imagination or a televised memory, Kyle had moved the standards, crossbar, and box into Sullivan gym. That way, the 1,400 students attending the afternoon rally could see just what an amazing feat one of their own had accomplished.

The high school pole vault standards at St. Ignatius were too short to match Mack's flight, so carpenters added a wooden extension on each side until the crossbar rested at 19 feet, 6¼ inches (5.95 meters). In Athens, under the pressure of the Olympic final, against the world's best, on his third and last attempt, Mack had gone where no man had gone before in Olympic history to clear that bar. Maybe only Mack could have felt at home, dwarfed by those extended uprights but ready to make the thin air the stuff of dreams.

He certainly knew his way around the weathered pole vault pit at the school. Years ago, you might have seen Mack rolling the standards out for practice with a hardy buddy or two in the dead of winter, brushing the snow off the runway, stripping off his coat and gloves until he had pared himself down to an efficient aerodynamic profile, and then, running toward the uprights, lowering the pole as he thundered closer. He would have seemed then a knight who was jousting with fear and failure, one who had been splintered by them more often than most competitors would have been able to endure. And finally, years later, after disappointment and defeat, he had succeeded wildly beyond all dreams except his own.

When the school assembly bell rang, students filed into the gym, an army of young boys in khakis, shirts, and ties. Many of them stopped in their tracks when they saw the towering uprights. Behind the pole vault pit, a huge drawing of Mack with the gold medal hung on the gym wall. You could see the students thinking: He did *what?* He went *how* high? Dude, do you get peanuts and a soft drink on a flight like that?

No one from Cuyahoga County, where Cleveland is located, had won an Olympic gold medal in an individual event since 1968 until Mack did it on August 27, 2004.

By the way, the Greek teacher finally translated the inscription, which was written in a dialect used in the sixth century B.C. The classical scholars translated it as: "Mistress of golden-crowned contests, Olympia, queen of the truth."

But the truth is no one saw this coming.

It's impossible to quantify brilliance precisely. As was once written, "you don't rate sunsets by their readings on a light meter." However, the pole vault is such a visually stunning event, its spectacle is so grand, that adding this literal measurement on the basketball court for all of the students and faculty to see to the very inch what Mack did in Athens, Greece, only made the tale taller.

In some ways, the pole vault conveys the meaning of competition more precisely than any other sport. It reflects both the idea of athletics as a ruthless meritocracy and society's hopes for improvement. Educators are always talking about raising the bar. Students are always seeking new heights. In pole-vaulting, you always know if you have succeeded or failed. But so many variables must be accounted for, so much energy is required, and so high is the fear factor that improvement comes in small increments.

Timothy Steven Mack is Exhibit A for the value of self-improvement, one hard-earned smidgen at a time. The comforting philosophy of progress, put to rout by the calamitous wars of the 20th century, scarred by the tracks of needles used to administer steroids and other performance-enhancers in track and field, finds its champion in him.

You don't have to be a prodigy like LeBron James or Tiger Woods. It's not what you were, but what you are that counts. Yet while winners sometimes cheat in track and field, no sport should be more removed from the "winning is the only thing" mentality. There are many, many more losers than winners in the sport. That's why PRs (personal records) are so important. They represent a melioristic view of the world. Things will get better. Improving oneself is the most important thing.

"It's an individual sport, and that intimidates some kids," said Kyle.

"They're fine if they're part of the football team or if they're on the relay. But it takes a special breed to lay it on the line when it's just you."

In the pole vault, there is no complaining that your teammates didn't throw you the ball; no griping about the run that would have gone all the way except for the missed block. Elite competitors have coaches, sports psychologists, and trainers. But at the most basic level, in the jump itself, it is all up to the pole-vaulter.

Pole-vaulters have a startling, sometimes contradictory blend of skills: speed enough in their last steps to be in the ballpark with sprinters, strength enough to make them the likeliest candidates to move the furniture in a room full of extreme sports participants like skateboarders, flexibility enough to rival the human pretzels in gymnastics, and, always, courage enough to dare.

Lean, swift and sinewy at 6-foot-2, 175 pounds, Mack, like all pole-vaulters, is overpowering in strength-to-weight ratio. His biceps are Popeye's after a spinach infusion. His upper body came from lifting over his lifetime a slag heap from the steel mills that once belched smoke into Cleveland's skies.

As for the courage, pole-vaulters all have it. They don't lift off from the runway without it. The pole vault is, per capita, the most dangerous school sport in America, and by a wide margin over football. A world-class skier once said, "A coward will never win the downhill." The same can be said about the pole vault. It seems to appeal to skywalkers with stars in their eyes, but no one turns himself into a catapult's payload without having gravel in his gut.

"There's a camaraderie in track and field, especially in the pole vault," said Kyle. "They respect each other's technique and training, and they respect each other's courage. It's almost a fraternity. When another pole-vaulter is on the runway, it's like they're bringing another brother into the lodge."

Mack came to the event not from an internal imperative to conquer his fears, although he was afraid of heights. He was drawn to the topsy-turvy world by default.

"It was," Mack said, simply, "something I was halfway decent at."

The quality that would take him to Athens was there even then. Tim Mack was the most persistent and least daunted kid in his neighborhood or any other. Like snow on the iron-hard ground of late fall in northern Ohio, like tape, like your shadow, he stuck to it.

"It's always been a part of me. I'd be in the batting cages for an hour at a time before baseball season. I would be out on the sidewalk when I started doing the pole vault, working on drills, working against the side of the house, doing it alone. I always had to prove myself. My back was always against the wall," Mack said.

Even then, he connected with coaches. These were the days before every child got to play in football, before every participant received ribbons in track and field, before self-esteem was held more valuable than excellence. When the coaches chose teams while Mack was in middle school, they almost always wanted "Timmy Mack" on their side. He had good hands, he took instruction well, and he wanted to improve like a fish wanted to swim.

He came to the pole vault because he was too small for football. He started out in the eighth grade, 13 years old, standing in a chair beneath the crossbar, holding a pole, visualizing the plant of the pole. His best height was 6 feet. It was the very bottom-most rung of a very tall ladder.

He left it for one year to play shortstop in baseball at St. Ignatius, but he didn't bat much, and he was one of the last players into the junior varsity games. The most complicated, demanding, expensive and perilous event in track and field became his specialty, because nothing else was.

There is absolutely nothing ordinary about committing body and soul to a flimsy pole that bends like a rainbow under a storm front. With your hands above your head, reaching for heaven, you hear a voice in your head screaming: "Surely this time it snaps like a twig and frags everybody in the neighborhood." And then you are performing thirty-two distinct muscular maneuvers in a half-second, while you hurtle upward, feet first, hanging on the pole like a bat in a cave. Your back is to the crossbar as you fly more blindly for a time than a pilot with the instrument panel on the blink and the landing strip socked in by fog.

"The pole vault is always the event decathletes are scared of," said Kyle. He was referring to the failure of Dan O'Brien, one half of Reebok's "Dan vs. Dave" ubiquitous commercials in 1992, to clear a bar ("no-heighting," as it is called) at that year's U.S. Olympic Trials.

"You can muscle some events," added Kyle, "but not the pole vault. You have to have the technique.

"But did I see greatness in Tim? To be honest, no. Tim was very good as a freshman, and he was going to be one of those guys who could really move up. I thought he might do 13 or 14 feet. Then he took the year off for baseball. I remember dragging the pole vault equipment out of the shed and seeing him in his baseball uniform, waving good-bye as the van pulled out."

The year away sent him back to vaulting, more determined than ever. "It was a blessing in disguise. He came back more dedicated. He had found something to latch onto," said Kyle.

In many ways, however, it was St. Ignatius that had latched onto him. St. Ignatius High School is a college preparatory school, a Jesuit school, and not a lot of corners are cut there. The Jesuits were the shock troops of the pope before that distinction went more appropriately to the right-wing Opus Dei. Organized basically to lead the Counter-Reformation, they were the Roman Catholic Church's intellectuals, known for their powers of reasoning and for their diplomacy. If there was an ecclesiastical beachhead to be taken, the Jesuits were the "Marines" whom the pope sent in. Former students at St. Ignatius are CEOs of companies all around Cleveland. The character B.D. from the comic strip *Doonesbury* was modeled on Brian Dowling, the quarterback at Yale in the 1960s. Dowling was a St. Ignatius man, class of 1964.

"I wouldn't be the person I am without going there," Mack said. "I had to work hard just to have a decent grade point average. I didn't want to fall below a 2.0. I struggled to get stuff done. See, school was not always for me. I knew I was going to graduate, but my attitude was, 'I don't want to fail a lot of classes.' College was a breeze for me after that. Preparing to pole vault was nothing like trying to keep my head above the water academically."

Part of the rigor came from Kyle, who also teaches English at the school. The text Chico Kyle really gets into is Ernest Hemingway's *The Old Man and the Sea*. When he speaks about the short novel, it is as if Kyle himself were in the rocking boat with Santiago, trying to keep the sharks away from the great marlin he has caught. "You know he's not going to make it back with the fish," Kyle said, "but he still puts up a great fight." Persistence, the book argues, has its own value. Hard work lends a kind of nobility to even the most thankless task. The fish isn't the trophy. The value isn't in the sea but in what the fisherman found inside himself.

Mack learned lessons from Kyle's books and from his home life. Tim

Mack was the youngest of the five children of Arlene and Don Mack. His father was the best punter in Cleveland while attending St. Ignatius in the 1950s. He played briefly at Notre Dame before winding up at John Carroll University. When the realty tax agency for which Don worked began to fail, he formed his own company and paid Catholic school tuition with sheer hustle. "I was 52 when I was let go. Oh, I was down in the dumps for a while, but I had friends among my old customers. I tried not to let on to Tim," said Don Mack.

Tim Mack once said his mother "keeps it real." By this, he meant she is not satisfied with poor performance and she does not brook excuses. There was a reason for that. Arlene Mack has coped with multiple sclerosis for twenty-five years. It forced her to give up the dog-grooming business she had in her home until Tim began the first grade, because the grooming shears became too heavy to hold in her weakened right hand. She had learned the trade by working for free for months at pet salons, clipping and shaving the animals, getting bitten once through the thumbnail, all so she could one day augment the family's income. Later, she worked in the marketing department of the real estate firm headed by Richard Jacobs, former owner of the Cleveland Indians. She kept her affliction a secret when she took falls. She made excuses when she had to give up racquetball and bowling. Arlene Mack was never one who wanted to be the object of sympathy. She now wears a brace on her right leg that corrects the drop foot condition that is a symptom of MS. The device helps her walk in a normal, heel-to-toe manner.

Arlene's illness is never completely out of Tim's mind. In 2006, a year and a half after his gold medal, her son would fly to parched, dusty Odessa, Texas, the hometown of Toby Stevenson. There, Mack and Stevenson, the high-flying rivals in Athens, Jeff Hartwig, the American record-holder, and Nick Hysong, the 2000 Olympic gold medalist, headed a contingent of pole-vaulters in a benefit meet to fund research into multiple sclerosis. Stevenson's mother Peggy died in 2008 from a more advanced form of MS than Arlene Mack. The pole-vaulters raised over $20,000 in donations and pledges at the Odessa event.

Mack's family was middle class, but the family's transportation system was not divisible by five children. So Tim Mack endured the small character-builders of having to ride his bike in football pads two miles to practice. "I'd get there and see all these other kids who had rides when they needed something," he said.

Since his birthday was in September, he was usually the youngest in his grade. He grew up a have-not, although not in the sense of grinding material deprivation. "I was the youngest and the smallest. The other kids got their size and coordination before me. I had to fight for everything I got," he said.

At St. Ignatius, he learned to fight for others as well. "The motto of St. Ignatius is 'Men for others.' All the people who worked with me gave the example to treat other people as I wanted to be treated. It sounds simple. But it's hard to do," said Mack.

The Prayer of Generosity of St. Ignatius Loyola says it best: "Lord, teach me to be generous. Teach me to serve you as you deserve; to give and not count the cost; to fight and not heed the wounds; to toil and not seek for rest; to labor and not ask for reward, except to know that I am doing your will. Amen."

You could find those values reflected in Tim Mack. Pole-vaulting was his passion, but it never became his identity. He would give his time to tutor friends spurned by their coaches. He would toil at menial jobs without rest, almost pursuing his athletic career in his spare time. For years, his rewards certainly weren't measured on a material scale.

The altruistic ideal is more difficult to detect in adolescents than in others. Parents at St. Ignatius check a list periodically to determine progress in being open to growth, intellectually competent, religious, and committed to justice.

The Jesuit goal is to create a sort of Catholic aristocracy, or maybe intellectual aristocracy. Still, as part of its commitment to reaching out to others, the school has remained at its inner-city, near–West Side location, resisting alumni calls to relocate to the suburbs. It's both a commitment to the urban community and a way of making students leave their suburban capsules. Perhaps it means that students from all over the Cleveland area get panhandled in an area that has seen better days, but maybe that is part of the education as well, a bump from the harder school waiting on the outside.

Mack's world grew wider there. As in life, some of what he encountered wasn't particularly pleasant. He learned from all of it.

"Tim always talks about being so lucky and having so many people support him," Kyle said. "But he's the kind of guy people like to be around. He's kind, sincere, soft spoken. Nobody doesn't like Tim."

Mack walls himself off from distractions at a meet, refusing to watch his competitors' jumps, intensifying his isolation. He lies on his back with his feet up, a visor keeping the sun off and tunneling his vision, the focus growing narrower until it finally reaches the pinpoints of light that are Mack's jumping "cues," which are seemingly dry, dull reminders about arm movement and posture. But Mack knew there were influences beyond his own skills lifting him up. In Athens, he called together his entire circle of family and friends after he won the gold medal and thanked them individually for helping to make it possible.

The gold medal had defined Tim Mack, for he would always be linked with the great track and field names of his hometown's past— Jesse Owens, a four-time gold medalist and one-man rebuke to Hitler's Master Race at the Berlin Olympics in 1936; Harrison Dillard, a two-time gold medalist and the only man to win the 100 meters and the 110-meter hurdles, in 1948 and 1952, respectively; and Madeline Manning, the 800 meters golden girl in 1968.

But it's what you do when you come down after clearing the bar that is in some ways even more important. Mack was always well grounded.

Tim Mack never made the high school state meet. His best jump at St. Ignatius was only a so-so 4.11 meters (13–5¾). This earned him a scholarship only to Malone College, a National Association of Intercollegiate Athletics (NAIA) school in Canton, Ohio. Today, the NAIA seems an athletic backwater, ignored by television. But Malone had a strong pole-vaulting program then, regularly dusting Notre Dame and other NCAA schools. Pole-vaulting at Malone beat the alternative Mack faced of walking on and competing without a scholarship at the University of Toledo, which didn't have a strong program.

At the high school rally for Mack, they showed a joke video of an old St. Ignatius teammate, Joe Zebrak, jumping in a dress shirt and tie and clearing "19–6¼." It was actually only 10 feet, and Zebrak sailed futilely beneath the crossbar when it was adjusted to an actual height of 15 feet. Many of his old teammates would not have been surprised if Mack had turned out to be just like Zebrak, a 9-to-5 guy who was a pretty good track and field athlete in his day.

When Mack was introduced at last, the student body rose in a standing ovation and so many small American flags fluttered in the stands that the Fourth of July seemed to have stolen a march on the calendar. Mack strode through the gym's rear door, holding the pole before him like Lancelot about to enter the tournament lists. A local boy had made good. He was a Clevelander, most of all. He had been defeated often, but it had never diminished him.

"Don't be afraid of defeat. It's okay to fail. But embrace it; don't run from it. Learn from it," he told the boys.

If ever anyone spoke to a crowd that had had a lifetime of opportunities to give defeat a hug, it was Mack to a Cleveland audience. Many of the boys had never seen a championship Cleveland team in a major professional sport, and the same could have been said about their fathers. The Browns' last NFL championship came in 1964. The Indians' last World Series championship came in 1948. The Cavaliers were swept in 2007 in their first trip to the NBA Finals.

It is natural in such a city to expect the worst. The Cavs might have won it all in the "Miracle of Richfield" year of 1976, except starting center Jim Chones broke his foot in practice the day before the conference finals against Boston began.

The Indians in 1997 became the first team ever to take a lead into the bottom of the ninth inning of the seventh game of the World Series and lose. The Browns not only lost in the 1980s, they lost in ways that ripped the heart out of the city and the franchise. There was the 98-yard fairy tale authored by John Elway in 1986. There was Earnest Byner's goal-line fumble in Denver the very next year. In Cleveland, the last two are simply known as "The Drive" and "The Fumble." In Cleveland, the fairy tale always ends with the big, bad wolf winning.

Even the Cavs, a distant third in popularity most years, got into the act in 1989, losing an epic first-round series to the Chicago Bulls on Michael Jordan's dagger to the heart at the final buzzer of the final game. It, of course, was known in Cleveland as "The Shot."

When a city commemorates defeat so regularly, it can lead to a climate of self-pity. The culture of victimization was everywhere in Cleveland by 2004. No city needed a champion more, even if it was one with dents in his armor from years of disappointment.

Tim Mack was different in that he never considered himself a victim. Mack had heights to climb and not depths to plumb. In a cloudburst, he comforted himself with thoughts of the coming rainbow.

"He is just a great, shining example of persistence," said Kyle. "So many people would have given up so many times. A big part of him is that he always stayed positive. He'd stop by school from time to time.

I'd ask how it was going, and it was never, 'I really screwed that meet up.' It was always optimistic. 'Oh, I'm working on a few things. I'm upbeat. It's coming together.'"

He didn't start with such equanimity. Like any other kid, he wanted gratification now, yesterday if possible. But the pole vault is not like gymnastics or figure skating, in which athletes hit their peak before the onset of puberty. Pole-vaulters slowly get the hang of the event. Bubka was an anomaly, winning the first of his six straight World Championships at the age of nineteen. For most pole-vaulters, however, the event is a struggle out of the old, bloody Greek dramas. "Over time, drop by drop, through suffering, we gain wisdom," the tragedian Aeschylus wrote in the fifth century B.C. No wonder frustration got the better of Mack for years.

In a Mack family video from his senior year, a young spindly Mack competed in a meet in Sandusky, Ohio. His mother long ago made herself a vaulting aficionado, and while watching the video across the years, she barked, "His hands are wrong" as he held the pole. When he rocked back on his heel to begin the sprint to the box, she murmured, "That's better."

The pole in the video looked like a plaything compared to the one he had brought to St. Ignatius. Its bend was slight, but then again the bar was low. Twice, Mack missed, and each time he fired the end of his pole into the runway afterward like an explorer claiming a distant land for his king. It was a forlorn territory he came to know very well.

Over time, drop by drop, Mack made use of the patient wisdom that comes from morning drives in the Cleveland winter when the salt trucks haven't been out, the Alberta Clipper is screaming down from Canada with its bone-chilling winds, and the traffic snarls would make Medusa's hair with its snake 'do look orderly.

"I'm very proud of being from that city. I very much consider myself a Cleveland guy. Hard-working, blue-collar. When I first took my girlfriend, Grace Upshaw, to Cleveland, I showed her the smokestacks," Mack said. "She's from California, so Cleveland was a whole new world. I told her, 'This is what Cleveland is about. This is what I'm about.' The city has had its heart broken so many times by its teams, but it hasn't lost its love for them."

After Mack's speech at his alma mater, he stood near the bleachers as the boys formed a line that wound almost all the way around the basketball court. He shook hands with every student who wanted to meet him. In his hometown, he was a great success. Indeed, he would win the award for Cleveland's Best Amateur Athlete for 2004. Mack is not really an amateur, but the category was created to give Olympic athletes recognition. He would never have beaten the winner of the award as Cleveland's Best Professional Athlete for 2004. That, of course, was LeBron James, a global celebrity before he was eighteen years old.

If Mack stood somewhat apart from his pole vault peers, Mack and the USA men's Olympic basketball were a study in contrasts. By the summer of 2004, it was a team to which no one was attaching the adjective "dream." The youngest team since the NBA players replaced collegians in 1992, it was also the least experienced in the professional era. The players were new to the international game and its rules. They symbolized to many the way basketball skills in the country of the sport's origin had atrophied, sacrificed on the altar of individual athleticism.

One of the key members of that Olympic team, LeBron James had entered the NBA as the most publicized rookie ever. He appeared on the cover of *Sports Illustrated* while he was a junior at Akron's St. Vincent–St. Mary High School under the screaming headline: "The Chosen One." As a senior, he was declared ineligible by the state high school governing board (a ban which was soon overturned by lawyers representing the school) for taking costly "throwback" jerseys from a sporting news store as gifts.

His future was already so bright, assured and imminent that his unemployed mother, Gloria, was able to use his potential NBA earnings as collateral to buy him some wheels for his 18th birthday. It wasn't just a car, but the biggest, baddest, in-your-face vehicle on the planet, a Hummer outfitted with three TV sets and leather upholstery embossed with the nickname King James.

Mack, who could have vaulted over it, was riding a borrowed bicycle while working on his master's degree.

When the Cavs won his draft rights in the lottery, it probably saved the franchise in Cleveland. By then, LeBron James was set for life. He signed a Nike sneaker contract for $90 million, plus a $10 million signing bonus, before he ever played a professional game. Coca-Cola, another global marketing giant, wanted a piece of him for its Sprite commercials.

So great was his fame, and so long was the reach of the NBA's marketing arm, that a reporter from Cleveland felt their touch in the dusty town of Megara, Greece, an hour's drive northwest of Athens, three days before the Olympic Games. Hassled by Greek Secret Service agents as he covered the leg of the Olympic torch relay run by a Greek-American from Cleveland, the reporter tried in vain to identify the hometown link that justified his presence on the sun-blistered road. He mentioned the Cleveland Browns and national champion Ohio State, only to be met by blank stares and shrugs of indifference.

"LeBron James? Cleveland Cavaliers?" the reporter said finally, mimicking a jump shot.

"Oh, I love NBA! What is LeBron really like?" shouted the Greek Secret Service man who had been giving him the third degree, as he wrapped his arm around the reporter's shoulders.

LeBron had that kind of name recognition. But if the Greek cop had wanted to meet a real American Olympian, it would have been a pole-vaulter.

The pole vault gratifies the American appetite for spectacle and still fulfills the austere Olympic ideal of commitment to excellence because nothing else will do.

There is to pole-vaulting almost nothing of instant gratification. It does not speak to the instinct for fame that is the engine driving such hit television shows as *American Idol.* The breezy, irresponsible disdain of basics typical of the Olympic basketball team cannot characterize pole-vaulting. An irresponsible pole-vaulter often is, chillingly, a dead pole-vaulter.

The slow-motion camera loves the pole vault the way NFL Films loves power sweeps on the "frozen tundra." The pole vault is what Baryshnikov would have done if he had sprinter's speed, what Evel Knievel would have done if he hadn't discovered motorcycles. Its relative obscurity has given the pole vault something of a cult appeal. It's the odds-on choice to elicit more "oohs" and "ahs" from fans than any other event in track and field. Yet a recent poll ranked track and field as America's twenty-fifth favorite activity. The explanation was fairly simple, according to Mack's great rival, Toby Stevenson. You can throw a football around with your buddies, throw a baseball around with your dad, or shoot baskets by yourself. It takes considerably more trouble to set up a pole vault pit.

All that the pole vault offered fans was a treehouse dream of freedom that is similar to the way a dunk makes a heaven of a playground. In fact, the very reason the pole vault exists is to raise the bar and make the spirit soar. Its objective is to take you higher. Pole-vaulters are sky pilots, trying to touch the sky.

In some ways, the basketball team, which scratched and scraped to win a bronze medal, seemed a grotesque mockery of the Olympic ideal of self-sacrifice. The players lived on a luxury cruise ship. Allen Iverson reported to "boot camp" in Jacksonville, Florida, in a stretch limousine that covered the distance from "ostentatious, if-you-got-it, flaunt-it" luxury to "possible symptom of megalomania."

Even the great prodigy, James, had a mechanical flaw in his jump shot, often fading backwards when he did not have to, which threw off his balance and kept his shoulders from "squaring up" to the basket.

A pole-vaulter would have no-heighted with such slipshod technique.

In the world of Olympic celebrities, Tim Mack was, literally, the other pole. He had sharpened his skills during years of toil, often in obscurity, without the guarantee of a sultan's lifestyle, before he ever competed in a single meet, without "street cred," driven solely by his own imperative to go higher.

When Mack and the Cavaliers met, the franchise made him a sideshow to a sideshow before the game began. In a way, it figured. The NBA is all too often about style, not substance. On December 21, 2004, the Cavs invited Mack to be the team's "sixth man" for a game against the Minnesota Timberwolves. Mack, an avid sports fan, quickly agreed. His parents bought four pricey seats only six rows behind the Cavs bench for themselves, Tim, and his young nephew.

Most sports fans, no matter their age, harbor a twelve-year-old inside them. The eternal twelve-year-old talked baseball in his day, Willie, Mickey and the Duke. He listened to daytime World Series games on a transistor radio, smuggled by the grade school Resistance into classrooms. That twelve-year-old never really goes away. He resurfaces in curiosity, in flaring sparks of interest, even in enthusiasms.

Pole-vaulting could have been an "I'm the king of the world!" moment at the top of the jungle gym, for the sports twelve-year-old in Cleveland today relates to LeBron and the air up there. The connection to Mack, however, was lost on the self-absorbed Cavaliers. They showed no highlights of the last-gasp gold medal, when Mack went up like a shooting star.

Mack had met James briefly at the Opening Ceremonies in Athens and had had his picture taken with him. "He didn't seem all that interested in talking," said Mack. In fact, James seemed most interested in socializing with Akron-born 200-meter female sprinter LaShaunte'a Moore.

The night of the game, Mack brought a digital camera with him and snapped pictures constantly. But he didn't get to meet with James at all. Before the game began, Mack stood a couple of feet from the baseline on the court, across from the Cavs' bench, and introduced himself. There was no caterwauling, rabble-rousing public address system intro for him, even though the team's public address announcer greets each Cavaliers starter as if he invented the electric light.

"I'm Tim Mack, the pole vault gold medalist at the Athens Olympics," Tim said. Then, his voice spiking, he cried: "Cavaliers fans! Are you readyyyyyyyy?"

And then the furry mascot, Moondog, raced onto the court, as the T-and-A show of the Cavs' cheerleaders danced in his wake. The house lights went off, and spotlights picked out every starter as he was introduced, with James' name drowned out by the roars. In the entire 20,562-seat arena, only Minnesota's Kevin Garnett, with a gold medal from the Sydney Games in basketball, had what Mack had.

"You have a gold medal, and he only has a bronze," a reporter said as Mack returned to his seat.

Mack smiled wistfully. "He has $100 million from Nike, though," he said.

He didn't want to seem ungrateful to the Cavs, so he said it wasn't a big deal that he didn't get to talk to James. Then Mack reached inside his Team USA jacket and pulled the gold medal out that hung from his neck. "I could have said, 'Hey, man. This is what one looks like,'" he said.

2 Daredevils

Almost alone among athletes, pole-vaulters slip the bonds of earth and gravity. Pole-vaulters began as Lost Boys who dreamed of flying with Peter Pan. The pole vault—the most technologically advanced, adventurous event of them all—represents all the innocence, bravado, and magic of childhood.

Baseball is always the beneficiary of idealized childhood memories, of summer and school's out, of green grass and high skies. Pole-vaulters seem to have enjoyed the same lyrical evocation of boyhood as Dylan Thomas described in the poem "Fern Hill." They were "young and easy under the apple boughs." From these boughs, the most colorful of them, the rambunctious, flamboyant Olympic gold medalist, Don Bragg, swung on ropes, screaming the falsetto war cry of Tarzan.

"When you really nail one," said Bragg, "it's almost mystical. You see it in segments instead of—whoosh—in a continuous flow. The swing. The rock back. The plant. The pull-up. On a great vault, you can look straight down the pole while doing a handstand on it. A flash goes off in your mind like a 35-millimeter camera."

"There was a picture of me in *Sports Illustrated* where the angle made it look like I was up there in the third balcony of Madison Square Garden," said the Rev. Bob Richards, one of the sport's first stars. "The caption said the pole vault is a symbol of human achievement, of jumping on a flimsy pole and trying to do the impossible. It said it was the symbol of the venturesome spirit."

Pole-vaulters don't always start with the nonchalance of stunt men. But it becomes a big part of them. Richards, who is on the short list of the greatest vaulters ever, evolved into being a pole-vaulter. It was a function of his all-around athletic ability.

"It's the greatest all-around event there is," said Richards. "I played all sports. I was all-state in Illinois in football and averaged nineteen points per game in basketball. But no sport captivated me like the pole vault. It builds your upper body like nothing else. You have to do sprints in it. You use the same takeoff as in the [pre–Fosbury Flop] high jump and long jump. I set decathlon records because of pole-vaulting."

Richards was world-ranked six times in the decathlon and three times was the American national champion in the ten-event competition. He never medaled in the event in the Olympics, finishing thirteenth in 1956, but he clearly had the ability to do so. No other pole-vaulter ever qualified for the Olympic decathlon.

Others came to pole-vaulting in the morning of their double-dog-dare-you youth. The air was their element. When they fell, it was not a punishment for their overweening pride—the sin that brought Icarus down in Greek myth, his wax wings melting as he flew too close to the sun. His story belongs on the dusty shelf of legend. In the spills from the garage roofs and apple boughs taken by young pole-vaulters, Icarus plunged then swam. Such events were the baptism of pole-vaulters, the anointing of their imaginative spirit. When they grew bigger, of course, they fell harder. Some of them died.

Pole-vaulters are off by themselves, separated from the rest of a track team by the rakish nature of their event. In the heights they reach, they make even high jumpers, with their backward rag-doll flops, seem gravity-bound. The pole-vaulters are all members of the same lodge: the Brotherhood of Big Air. As Arthur Miller wrote of a salesman's imperative to dream, so a man with a pole has got to dare. Both come with the territory.

"You have the sprinters over here and the relay team over there; the big guys, the throwers are in their rings; and off by themselves in a corner of the field are the vaulters, the daredevil pilots at twelve o'clock high," said Chico Kyle, Mack's high school coach.

Sprinters preen and strut. Maurice Greene once had a friend spray his spikes with a fire extinguisher after the 100m dash. But pole-vaulters respect the game. A man can lose a lot more than a medal up there. And yet pole-vaulters are rebels, the cockeyed, asymmetrical, off-center individualists. "At the Pole Vault Summit," Mack said, referring to an early-season meet and symposium held in Reno, Nevada, "they're always telling us, 'You are daredevils! You are stunt men!'" They are risktakers off the track, too. Mack, for example, plays Texas Hold 'em poker, slot machines, and roulette.

"A track coach told me once that it was easy to find pole-vaulters," said Bragg, the 1960 Olympic gold medalist. "Maybe he was doing a presentation at school and there might be one kid at the back of the room who was standing with one foot on the back of his desk, ready to jump from it to the top of another desk. 'There's my pole-vaulter!' the coach would yell."

In some ways, Bragg's name became his life story. He's outrageous and outsized, self-described in his autobiographical book entitled *A Chance to Dare* as a "butt-end-of-everything kid from the New Jersey swamplands." At Villanova, he steered the same kind of paths as the Delts at Faber College in *Animal House*. Double-secret probation was never more than an escapade away.

He and Richards, a theology professor and ordained minister, will always be linked because, as Bragg said, "We had almost a father-son relationship." They were the premier pole-vaulters of the 1950s, when space flight was still a dream and the Cold War gave even athletic competition a militaristic cast. They represented a changing of the guard in the sport. Richards learned from Cornelius Warmerdam, the master of the bamboo pole. Bragg was the last champion to ride steel.

Bob Seagren followed as the sport entered a New Frontier of fiberglass. He was movie-star handsome and almost as wild-ass crazy as Bragg. In 1968 he won the Olympic gold medal. It was the sixteenth in a row for America and the last for thirty-two years. Even as the pole vault became an Eastern European–dominated sport filled with esoteric training regimens and suspicions of doping, Seagren both legitimized the event and popularized it with his countrymen. Ironically, it was accomplished in a made-for-television exhibition that is remembered as the first of a long line of "trash sports."

Cornelius Warmerdam will never get his due. On the bamboo pole, he could fly like the Man of Steel. He was the Babe Ruth of the event in his era. Without question, Warmerdam is one of the ten greatest track and field athletes of all time. Interestingly, Warmerdam won no Olympic gold medals, perhaps only because there were no Olympics in his heyday. World War II wiped out the Olympics in 1940 and 1944.

Warmerdam learned to vault in a cabbage patch outside Fresno, California, in what can only be called the "Dead Pole Era." Using bamboo, he set the type of records that should have belonged to the distant future. In 1940 Warmerdam became the first to clear 15 feet, or 4.57 meters. He accomplished that feat forty-three times in his career and set a record of 15-7¾ (4.77) that lasted fourteen years. No one else cleared 15 feet until Richards in 1951. Warmerdam retired in 1944 with a record height 9 inches (23 centimeters) better than his closest competitor. This is an astonishing feat when you consider the current record holder (Sergey Bubka) can claim only 10 centimeters (4 inches) as his margin.

Richards barely knew Warmerdam when he called him in Fresno, California, where "Dutch" became an outstanding track coach. "I was a foot below his record," Richards said, "so I said to him, 'Dutch, can you help me? I can't get any higher.'"

For three days, Warmerdam worked with Richards. "He was a symbol of all the Dutch qualities, including high integrity," said Richards. "Did you know that at the age of seventy he set a world record for his age?

"I had leveled off at 14–6 [4.42], so I went out to Fresno, and he shared his wisdom with me. I remember he asked me why I gave up on bamboo. Well, I thought I needed a stiffer pole," Richards said. "That was the wisdom of the day. Stiffer was better, we thought. But he thought bamboo would give me more pop, more of a kick to get his record."

Richards wrote a famous essay based on his relationship with Warmerdam for the *Chicken Soup for the Soul* series. It was called "Greatness Is All Around You—Use It." It is a sunny, optimistic view, invoking the generosity of Warmerdam's competitive spirit.

"Great people will share. Great people will tell you their secrets,"

Richards insisted. "Go where they are. It's easy to be great when you're around great people."

The Vaulting Vicar

An athlete was nothing in Richards' day without a nickname. His ministry led him to be called the "Vaulting Vicar." "The Pole-vaulting Parson" was another popular one.

"I never, ever believed any of the stuff people said that God wanted me to win the Olympics," Richards said. "The kingdom of God is within you. God wants you to do your best. In my case, that was to be the best pole-vaulter, the best student, the best speaker. A Congressman once told me that God must have held the pole for me. Wasn't that silly? The idea that God was interested in who won the pole vault?"

Just going by the hardware, Richards is the greatest pole-vaulter ever. He is the only repeat Olympic gold medalist (1952 and '56). Richards also won a third medal, a bronze, in 1948. He was almost unbeatable indoors, winning the Millrose Games in New York eleven straight times. It is a remarkable record for a man whose body, superbly conditioned as it was, took a fearsome beating from the toll of falling from 15 feet into a pit filled with sawdust, if he were lucky, or often hard-packed sand if he were not.

He also beat back the challenge of the first fiberglass poles.

"That fiberglass pole was a whole new thing in the sport," Richards said. "It was a revolutionary change. It put 4 or 5 more feet [in height] on the thing. And that's when the dangerous aspects came into the sport."

Novice pole vault observers might think poles snapping as vaulters catapult toward the sky pose the greatest danger, but improved technology and stricter weight-ratio rules have dramatically lessened the incidence of broken poles. Today, missed landings are the sport's gravest danger.

"When I vaulted with a stiff metal pole, you never missed the pit," Richards said. "I could tell you to a spot the size of a washrag where I was going to land. But you take fiberglass, which acted like a spring, a highly explosive force, and you ride it—that's a different animal. That's something you need a lot of experience to do."

In 1956 Richards should have been beaten by Georgios Roubanis of Greece, who used the first fiberglass pole in Olympic pole-vaulting competition. Roubanis improved his personal best by 3½ inches (9 cm) but settled for the bronze medal. Roubanis got great lift, but he had not mastered the trajectory of the newfangled gadget and kept coming down on the crossbar rather than behind it. Richards needed his third and last try in 1956 to clear a shockingly low 13–1½ (4.00) in qualifying. The final in Melbourne, Australia, forced him to summon all the resources of a dedicated career plus a dollop of pure, dumb luck.

"The runway was patchy. It was made of brick dust, and we were all struggling," said Richards. "It came down to me and Bob Gutkowski, and the bar was at 14–11½ (4.56). The wind was in our faces, and I hit the bar going over [on his second attempt]. That bar bounced and bounced. It hung on the pegs by one-quarter of an inch, and it was hanging down then. I lay there in the pit with my hands together as if praying, thinking, 'Oh, God. It's coming off.' There is no question in my mind that the wind held it on."

It was not the first time he defied the odds. "I had pulled my Achilles tendon in '56, and it affected my takeoff in the jumps in both the decathlon [where he finished thirteenth] and pole vault," Richards said. "In Helsinki in '52, I pulled a hamstring. The first fiberglass pole certainly should have been the end of my streak in '56."

Great as he was on the runway, Richards might have been greater off it. A foe of Cold War stereotyping, he became a proponent of Olympic inclusiveness. His was not a spy vs. spy world of East vs. West but one of athletes without borders. In 1952 athletes from the former Soviet Union were allowed to compete for the first time. It was easy to cast the Olympians as surrogate warriors and the medal race as a contest to decide which political system was superior. Richards was having none of it. He led a delegation of American athletes across the Athletes Village to meet with their Soviet counterparts.

"I was accused of being too friendly with the Soviets," Richards said. "I'm sure it was contrary to what Josef Stalin wanted. You see, the athletes respected each other when they got the chance to talk. There's no question sports can break down barriers. Look at the ping-pong team that went to what was then called Red China. Look at the influence of the gymnasts. Every little girl in this country wanted to be Olga Korbut or Nadia Comaneci. There is something bigger in sports than borders or medal races."

"What became obvious," said Richards, "is that they didn't like the system. The Soviet athletes told us that in broken Spanish and in English and in Russian. They had no freedom. They lived in fear. Stalin's technique was to call you in and say that if you confessed to being a traitor, he would only kill you and not your family too. How can a system like that ever last?"

Richards encouraged the Russian jumpers by shouting "Harosho!" ("good") on their clearances, and they in turn cheered "Bootiful!" when he sailed over a bar. After he won in Helsinki, two Soviet pole-vaulters ran over to embrace him. The subsequent photograph became a world symbol of idealism in sports.

"I sent the first fiberglass poles to the Russians," he said. "It was before the first USA-Russia dual track meet in 19[58], because they couldn't get any good ones. Boy, did that ever boomerang on the USA!"

Richards was closely identified with the better aspects of sports: clean competition and respect in spite of political ideologies. "It was what I believed," Richards said. "If you study the Olympic ideology in ancient times, it was beautiful. They laid down their arms and held a peaceful competition. It was highly religious, and much of it was predicated on strength. Hercules was the patron god."

Richards is the patriarch of pole-vaulting's highest flying family. His son Brandon held the national high school record for thirteen years. "We still hold the family record," he said of the various jumping Richardses. "I think we're up there around 90 feet cumulative in highest bars cleared, and I have a couple of grandkids who are going to be good too."

Ironically, Richards wants to stand athwart the path of progress as far as the fiberglass pole goes and cry: "Halt!" He worries that with poles costing $500 each and pits costing over $10,000 schools are no longer going to be able to afford the sport.

"Besides the cost effectiveness, people are dying in the sport," Richards said. "I really think they're going to have to go back to the steel pole. I used a $30 stiff pole and went to two Olympics with it."

In 1984 Richards ran for president on the ultra–right wing Populist Party ticket. When he realized a cabal of neo-Nazis and former Ku Klux Klan members ran the party, he virtually stopped campaigning out of embarrassment.

After his Olympic success, Richards became a spokesman for Wheaties. He was the first to appear on a box. Getting your picture on a

Wheaties box today is the ultimate expression of Americana, keying into heartland values, connoting amber waves of grain and clean-cut, God-fearing manliness. The judging controversy in Olympic gymnastics, thought eventual winner Paul Hamm of the United States, might have hurt him most of all by costing him a Wheaties box appearance.

"Sure, I still eat them," said Richards, now living on a ranch in Gordon, Texas, 50 miles west of Fort Worth. "A bowl of Wheaties every day and about 10,000 hours of hard work can take you anywhere you want to go in life."

TARZAN

It happened in Istanbul, but it could have been almost any place where Don Bragg pole-vaulted—just another tale in the 1,001 tales of his life. In 1958, while Bragg was enjoying an evening on the town in Islamic Istanbul during a Eurasian tour, a rich sheik and his entourage cut in on Bragg and a woman with whom he was dancing. Understandably miffed and not bound by the finer points of diplomatic protocol, Bragg and his buddies bull-rushed the Turks and scattered them like tenpins. They then hailed a cab, returned to their hotel, and pushed heavy furniture against the door to keep out the sheik's scimitar-wielding henchmen.

In *A Chance to Dare,* Bragg wrote that he apologized to the coach of the American team and said he didn't know why he kept getting in trouble. "Hell, son," the coach said, patting him on the shoulder. "You're crazy. That's all."

The coach provided an explanation, but further evidence came from the times Bragg dove off bridges, leaped out of a powerboat, nearly stepped on a deadly black mamba snake, almost swam into the maw of a turbine, plummeted from the rafters into a swimming pool, tried to turn himself into a charcoal briquette when his pole hit a power line, arm-wrestled and beat the strongest man in Iraq, became a prototype for the Harlem Globetrotters and the Peace Corps, and otherwise cut an outrageous swath through the stuffy world of amateur track and field in the 1950s. Much of this Bragg did while bellowing like Tarzan, the make-believe noble primitive whom he idolized. Bragg never got to play Tarzan on the silver screen, but he spent his boyhood looping tree limbs with ropes, and he made his life an audition for the role.

The sense of purity and freedom he felt when swinging on his "vines" tapped an atavistic memory of a time when trees were the greenhouse of man. He could only recapture the feeling with the rare air of a soaring vault.

His training ground was similar to that of Warmerdam. Bragg grew up in a mostly black neighborhood in the so-called Cabbage Patch area of Penns Grove, New Jersey. They grew cabbages in the fields, and it always smelled like St. Patrick's Day. Like Mack, he was a pole-vaulter who feared heights. Mack is so technically efficient, his numbers so precise, his approach so methodical that he seems to fill the time with busy work and the click of abacus beads. But really, it was just the same as Bragg. Both jumped as a way of plunging into what they were afraid of and mastering it.

"I still have a fear of heights," Bragg said. "I can't stand on a third-story hotel balcony without getting dizzy, without experiencing vertigo like you wouldn't believe. It has to do with the inner ear. But I dived off cliffs and off bridges anyway. It was a way of conquering fear. I was going to do it. They were not going to scare my ass. And I always had a little problem with authority figures."

"I can't do what?" Bragg added, mimicking a conversation with his old college coach, James "Jumbo" Elliott of Villanova. "And all of a sudden I'm on a rafter above the pool at Villanova, and I'm jumping in."

He saw height as an expression of freedom from knowing his place, from the suffocation of society's rules. When he would go shooting untrammeled across the sky, he was at last high above the stunted little men who ran sports and grubbed at their work in the dark. Bragg seldom hid his scorn for autocratic U.S. Olympic Committee (and later IOC) head Avery Brundage. In his mind, Olympics officials were the types of people that preferred hotels Lord Greystoke would have patronized. The jocks got ape-man accommodations.

The Tarzan fixation that dated to the moment he saw Weissmuller play the part when he was eight years old helped Bragg develop his upper body as he swung on ropes throughout his childhood. Pole-vaulters must have a high strength-to-weight ratio because, obviously, a larger man has more to lift. Bragg was one of the heavier vaulters, at nearly 200 pounds. He sometimes would "kink" the poles, his weight putting a crimp in the metal. He broke twenty-seven poles that way.

"Everything changed with fiberglass," Bragg said. "It's much more precise now. If your steps are off even just a little bit, it affects your takeoff, and the whole vault is in trouble. Timing is much more critical. Strength was a bigger part of it in my day."

He vaulted like Tarzan penduluming through the jungle. If he could have thumped his chest and still handled the pole, he would have. He tore his body up. He experienced what is called "shoulder shock." The joints took the jolt of the plant of the steel pole. Fiberglass would transfer some of this force to the pole. He had the requisite guts too. Bragg has had two spinal operations because of the battering he took falling into sand-filled landing pits. And despite all that, he loved it so.

"Who else but a crazy man is going to put himself through all that, flying around up there at the mercy of a skinny pole?" Bragg said.

In Bragg's era, the pole vault almost stood alone. "Oh, it was a premier event," said Bragg. "There was the mile, the 100, depending on the quality of the sprinters, and the pole vault." Today, track and field as a whole has declined in popularity in the United States, but the pole vault's popularity within the sport is essentially unchanged since Bragg's day.

A bent pole took Bragg all the way from Penns Grove to the glittering capitals of Europe and the veils and sultanates of the Middle East.

"I jumped all over Europe," he said. "I even jumped in Baghdad. Baghdad! What's happening there now must be because of all the good-will I created."

"I jumped 14–6," Bragg added. "Then I stopped because I was falling into hard-packed sand. The coach comes over and says nobody ever jumped 15 feet in Iraq. I said, 'Nobody's going to either.' I went over and threw the shot then arm-wrestled their champion. Arm-wrestling is very big in Iraq. I didn't exactly feel the love when I beat him."

Bragg struck up friendships with Soviet athletes, particularly pole-vaulter Vladimir Bulatov and long-jumper Igor Ter-Ovanesian. His passport was stamped in all the languages of Babel. "We went all over the world. In many ways, we were the first Harlem Globetrotters," he said. "Sometimes, when we got back, we were debriefed by the government. They saw the good we could do with ordinary citizens, and that led eventually to the Peace Corps."

Often, he chased Richards around the world. If anything emphasizes the difference between them, it might be their separate visits to Sri Lanka, the former Ceylon.

"Oh, it was a grand time," said Richards. "I got carried off on the shoulders of the people. Everybody was singing 'Home on the Range.' The consulate said nothing had affected the people there like that. I asked them, 'Weren't you trying to make friends with these people or what?'"

"Wherever I went, Bob Richards had the record," said Bragg. "The conditions in Sri Lanka were very inferior, the pits, the runway, but that was usual. I cleared 14–4 [4.37], and I figure I've got to break Richards' record of 14–6, so we set the bar at 14–7 [4.45]."

In those days, it was a miss if the pole passed under the bar, even if the jumper cleared. Josh Culbreath, one of Bragg's friends, stood near the standards ready to catch the pole.

"I'm on the runway," continued Bragg, "and all of a sudden over the rim of the stadium come these huge flying bats. They were fruit bats or some damn thing. Everybody takes cover and, zoom, they fly by. I get up to try again, and here comes another squadron of them on another strafing run. They're swooping down, so I start running for it. Josh has already taken cover, and he's yelling, 'Get 'em, Tarzan! Tarzan's not afraid of anything!'"

Carting poles around is a pole-vaulter's occupational hazard. Every man who ever competed in the event has stories of airlines misplacing poles, refusing to take poles, shipping poles by mistake to Sri Lanka. But Bragg could have been killed in Philadelphia when his pole touched a power line while he was trying to slither, angle, and wedge it into a trolley at the 30th Street Station. A man who gets a second chance at life after such a moment often feels he has been saved for a higher purpose. Bragg, however, already felt he had been born and reborn through countless cycles of life and death.

At Rome, when he won the gold medal in the 1960 Olympics, he felt he had been in the Coliseum in a previous life and that he had suffered terribly before dying as a gladiator. He could put himself in a trance-like state then go back to the blood and the dust, his limbs shaking, his body thumping on the bed.

"I wrote a poem called 'Being,'" he said.

The entity, the representation of incandescence
It comes to me in its primordial essence.
The only necessity to change is the scenery.
I continue to pole ride with the spirits of the past.

"Do I believe in reincarnation?" he continued. After a long pause, Bragg said: "Unquestionably." He won the gold medal, he felt, because he was a warrior come back to the arena he knew, because he had a "home-field advantage."

"If any of those guys who went to Greece had any greater spiritual experience than I did in Rome, then they're God," said Bragg.

He thought he could live forever in the tree house, jumping in the dappled light, daring the green roof of the world, jumping until the poles gave out. But he couldn't, of course. He has been plagued by health and financial problems in his old age. He lost many of the mementos of his career in a fire. He developed gout (a not-unheard-of problem for athletes who subsisted on a high-protein diet for years), suffered two heart attacks, and overcame alcoholism. After all that, Bragg often wonders why he was spared electrocution.

"I figure God said, 'I'm going to keep him alive until his ass gets over that bar, then I'm going to throw all kinds of shit and lightning bolts at him and see how he can dance,'" Bragg said.

By the 1960 Olympics, he was drawing a private's pay in the U.S. Army. In a special pre-Olympics edition of the game show *What's My Line?* Bragg was scheduled to appear, along with the American track and field Olympic coach, hammer thrower Albert Hall, and Olympic legend Jesse Owens as the mystery guest. But the show ran out of time, and Bragg was merely introduced at the end with an underline identifying him as an Army private. He did not get to play a game.

After his medal ceremony, Bragg broke loose with a Tarzan yell. The people who ran the International Olympic Committee were not amused.

The old gladiator also never got to play Tarzan in the movies. A lawsuit stopped the filming of Bragg's movie *Tarzan and the Jewels of Opar* in 1964, and a fire later destroyed the prints. Perhaps, though, he lived the part in life's jungles.

Although he bears the scars of an I-dare-you life, he can still bust that defiant tremolo he practiced from the treetops. Asked if he can still do a Tarzan yell, he said from his home in Clayton, California: "Better hold the phone away from your ear." The scream that followed would have won Jane and Cheetah's hearts forever.

"Small children are running outside their houses," Bragg said upon finishing, "and all the dogs in the neighborhood are howling."

Bob Seagren took magic carpet rides. Well, sort of. He was eleven years old, fooling around with his older brother back in Pomona, California, and the bamboo poles around which department stores wrapped rugs became for him both a method of conveyance and, later, a career choice.

"The first couple of years, I never used it for height. It was a mode of transportation," he said. "We'd move from the roof of one garage to another, see who could go the furthest without touching the ground and things like that. I missed a bunch of times, but I never got hurt seriously."

He would go skylarking around the whole neighborhood, tree to roof, roof to roof, tree to tree, jumping and vaulting until he seemed almost arboreal in nature.

"Even though we got around the block pretty good, I literally got clotheslined once," said Seagren. "I was trying to jump over the clothesline my mother hung the wash on and caught the wire on my neck. It tore all the skin off. I had trouble swallowing for a few days."

Seagren came from the daredevil tradition of pole-vaulting, but he seemed a breed apart from earnest Midwesterners like Richards or hardscrabble guys from Jersey like Bragg. He went to the University of Southern California, where celebrated coach Vern Wolfe made him part of a stable of Trojan Olympians. Wolfe coached such Olympic gold medalists as Dallas Long in the shot put, Donald Quarrie in the 200 meters, Rex Cawley in the 400 hurdles, Randy Williams in the long jump, and Seagren, the 1968 Olympic pole vault champion. He also coached O.J. Simpson, who ran on a USC team that still holds the world record for the no-longer-performed 440-yard relay.

"I resented Seagren at first," said Bragg. "I was pissed off at the fiberglass pole. It took me twelve years to get the world record on the steel pole, and then along comes fiberglass, and these guys fresh out of college, and it becomes gymnastics moves, not strength. The records just went crazy."

A key to Seagren's success was that Wolfe was one of the earliest proponents of strength training. Even in the 1950s at North Phoenix High School in Arizona, Wolfe was urging his athletes to lift weights. He took empty cans, filled them with cement, connected them with rods, and thus created instant barbells. Many athletes in that era, aside from bodybuilders and weightlifters, eschewed lifting, thinking it would make them too muscle-bound.

While weights developed the strength Seagren needed, the requisite courage he already had from his aerial transits of the old neighborhood. "It never entered my mind that it was dangerous, although the fiberglass poles were pretty new then," he said. "I must have had twenty or thirty of them break. I was never hurt, although the fragments of the pole hurt people standing around me."

Every pole-vaulter faces trials. Seagren just happened to face two in one Olympic season. It was the beginning of his estrangement from the officials who ran amateur track and field.

"They said the winner of the Trials was assured of a spot for Mexico City in 1968 and that second and third would be picked after that in a meet at Lake Tahoe," recalled Seagren, the winner of the first Trials. "Then, they changed their minds and said the whole team would be picked at Tahoe. In between, I got hurt. They had some tune-up meets at Lake Tahoe, and I went up there the Saturday before the big meet and hurt my back warming up."

Seagren had pinched a nerve. He would lie flat on his back in a hospital bed that had been stiffened by a board placed under the thin mattress. He took Demerol to dull the pain every two hours. He was back in the shantytown of trailers in which the athletes were housed by the middle of the next week. He won the second Trials, setting a world record of 17–9.

But the game had changed. Seagren's most excellent adventures and his most strident controversies were overshadowed by political developments—in 1968, the Tommie Smith/John Carlos black-gloved protest of racial injustice in America, in 1972, the terrorist massacre of Israeli athletes.

Seagren was only twenty-one when he won the gold medal at 17–8½ (5.40), when a three-way tie came down to fewest misses. In Mexico City, he was a member of perhaps the greatest track team ever assembled with Lee Evans in the 400, Bob Beamon in the long jump, Jimmy Hines in the 100, and Smith in the 200 all setting formidable records there, while Dick Fosbury revolutionized the technique of the high jump with the international debut of the "Fosbury Flop."

But as the pole vault final neared its conclusion, Smith, the winner of the 200, and Carlos, the bronze medalist, staged their medal ceremony protest during the playing of the "Star-Spangled Banner."

Ten days before the Olympics began, on October 2, 1968, a crowd of 5,000 students had gathered in Mexico City's Plaza of the Three Cultures to protest the Mexican government's vast expenditures on fun and games in an impoverished nation. Soldiers and police shot and killed an estimated 200 of them. In June of 1968, Robert F. Kennedy had been assassinated. In April of the same year, Martin Luther King Jr. had been assassinated. In that time and in that place, the protest Smith and Carlos made against America's institutionalized racism and, by implication, the misplaced priorities of waging a war in Vietnam amid such inequities at home was heard 'round the world.

It created a sensation to which Seagren, wrapped in his cocoon of concentration, was almost immune.

"All I knew was we were jumping for a world record [of 17–10½, or 5.45]," Seagren said. "The protest never entered my mind. I had great tunnel vision. Exterior things went away. You really had to have blinders on, because the focus is so intense, and it has to remain so intense for so long."

"We had started warming up at noon," he added. "Warm-ups were a big deal. They were a way to intimidate people. You wanted to nail practice jumps and let them know, 'You're all jumping to beat me.' I didn't take my first jump until 3:30 and didn't jump again until 5. The whole thing lasted seven and a half hours."

Seagren never had a problem with the protesters: "A lot of people misunderstood what they did. They meant no disrespect to the national anthem. I knew what inequities the black athletes faced back at home. They were under tremendous pressure to boycott, but most of them thought it was a once in a lifetime opportunity, and they had to go."

Four years later at Munich, embittered by the controversy that unseated him as pole vault champion (ending the Americans' century-long dominance of the event) and sickened by the ghastly terrorist massacre of the Israeli national team, he wondered if the Olympics themselves would continue.

"It made you think," Seagren said. "I wondered if Munich was the end of the Olympic movement. This was before 1984 [when the Los Angeles Olympics turned a profit], and every city that held them lost so much money. They had gotten so huge, they were almost impossible to police. I really thought this might be the last Olympics."

His own experience in the pole vault assured him that it was his final Olympics. Seagren lost because the governing bodies of track and field then had the same absolute control of athletes as medieval barons had over their serfs. "Citius, altius, fortius" is the Olympic motto. "Faster, higher, stronger—but only if we say so," should have been the motto.

The new fiberglass Cata-Pole, used by Seagren and all the top Americans, was ruled illegal on the eve of the competition despite the fact that the rules governing the pole vault said the implements can be made out of anything. The excuse was that the poles were not available to the Eastern Bloc athletes for twelve months before the Olympics. No such requirement existed in the rule book. It was a Luddite impulse, an attempt to reverse the course of technology, to smash the spinning jennies and return to the days of the distaff and spindle. At the 1972 Olympics, after the record book revolution that had been wrought by fiberglass poles in 1964 and 1968, reactionaries disciplined the sport. But they couldn't tame the sky for long.

"They made up the rules as they went along," said Seagren. "That was where I had the pleasure of making the acquaintance of Adriaan Paulen."

A Norwegian official of the IAAF and the organization's future president, Paulen was what Alabama governor George C. Wallace's "pointy-headed bureaucrats" wanted to be when they grew up—a pig-headed ignoramus with no scruples about fair play at all, unless they were provided for in Addendum 5, Paragraph 4, Clause 3, Appendix B to the actuarial tables.

"He really didn't have any criteria for what constituted a legal pole," said Seagren, "so he shot from the hip. Paulen and a West German coach were taking the butt plugs out of my poles and weighing them on a very unsophisticated bathroom scale."

Paulen and his aides discovered that some of the Cata-Poles were almost fifty grams lighter than the old-style poles, all of which were within ten grams of each other in weight. Fifty grams is less than two ounces, ten grams is less than a half-ounce. In essence, Paulen was debating the weight of gossamer vs. the heft of cotton candy. He was making war on people who broke the wrong end of the egg. He was as nearly a complete putz you would find anywhere else this side of the International Olympic Committee.

"I said if a pole is designed for a 180-pound man at 16 feet, 6 inches in length, that's what it weighs," Seagren said. "I said if the pole weighs six pounds, did he really think a matter of a couple of ounces made any difference? I said did he really think anyone could tell?"

According to Seagren, Paulen said: "One more word, and I'm throwing you out for unsportsmanlike conduct."

Seagren vaulted with an unfamiliar pole and finished second at 17–8½ behind East Germany's Wolfgang Nordwig at 18–0½ (5.50). Nordwig had struggled with the Cata-Poles, which might explain why East Germany filed the first protest against their use. Pole-vaulters seldom fare well on borrowed poles when their own are lost, so Seagren's silver medal was a tribute to his competitiveness and adaptability.

Afterward, Seagren snarled at Paulen, "You gave me this pole, now I'm returning it." Then, Seagren—Wham, with the right hand!—nearly gutted the official when he threw the pole at him.

"If I had shoved it where I wanted to, I'd still be in a German jail," said Seagren.

Fed up with the "shamateurism" of the day, he turned pro with the International Track Association, a circuit that lasted four years and featured world record-holders Jim Ryun (mile) and Randy Matson (shot put) in addition to Seagren.

At the mercy of their cumbersome implements, burdened on trips to meets with more baggage than anyone since Dorian Gray, pole-vaulters could have remained as they were before Seagren—a different breed admired for their aspirations to flight yet underappreciated for their ability as athletes in their event. Then came the original *Superstars* in 1973, a made-for-television sports event that captivated fans, made Seagren $39,700 richer as its first winner, and legitimized pole-vaulters as all-around athletes. ABC-Television, which had lost the contract to televise the NBA to NBC, seized on the concept as a drowning man might a lifeline. Its executives saw the show as programming to fill the gaps the loss of hoops had created in the young, male, beer-drinking, car-buying demographic marketing sector all networks targeted.

On the show, every athlete was a star in his own sport: Joe Frazier, boxing; Johnny Unitas, football; Johnny Bench, baseball; Elvin Hayes, basketball; Rod Laver, tennis; Rod Gilbert, hockey; Jean-Claude Killy, skiing; Peter Revson, auto racing, as well as the heir to the Revlon cosmetics empire; Jim Stefanich, bowling; and Seagren, a late addition.

"First, [jockey] Bill Shoemaker was going to be in it, but he broke his ankle in a race," said Seagren. "I called and was told they had other alternates lined up. They said they had bigger names, and they weren't interested in me. Then [golfer] Gary Player came down with appendicitis, and I was in."

Bench had had lung surgery to remove a benign tumor only months before the filming. Unitas was near the end of his career. The stars could not compete in their own sport. Seagren won the baseball hitting contest, the half-mile run, and the bike race on the last day to hold off runner-up Killy. Thanks to his USC coach's insistence on weight training, Seagren outlifted Frazier, who was approximately thirty pounds heavier but had never hoisted anything but his dukes.

Competitively, the *Superstars* featured Frazier going through the water like an anchor in swimming. "I really thought Howard Cosell was going to jump in and rescue him," said Seagren of the ABC broadcaster. "Frazier had never swum, and when I asked him why on earth he would choose swimming for one of his events, he said, 'I watched the others.'"

Frazier's view was that the athletes were delivering combinations worthy of the squared circle to the pool. "He was throwing lefts and rights at the water, but he wasn't going anywhere," said Seagren, laughing. "He was sinking like a rock."

To this day, Seagren, who runs a company that stages road races for runners and lives in Long Beach, California, gets recognized more for *Superstars* than anything else. After *Superstars* came a long parade of imitators, from *Battle of the Network Stars* up to the *Lingerie Bowl*. The publicity that came with the *Superstars* victory, along with his matinee idol looks, made acting a natural choice for Seagren's second career. He did several episodes of *Love Boat* and appeared on *Fantasy Island, Emergency,* and *Adam 12.* His most remembered role was as Dennis Phillips, a gay quarterback on the brilliant parody of afternoon television shows, *Soap.*

"I had always played jocks or coaches," Seagren said. "My agent told me I was playing a football player, and my thought was, 'Oh, great.' Then he told me he was gay, and my thought was, 'Uh-oh.' It was a different era, but I thought, 'Why not? It might make people think.'"

After *Soap,* Seagren toiled on through seven failed pilots, in most of which he was required to remove his shirt and serve as eye candy for the female audience.

"*Stunt Seven* was one of them," he said "We were stunt men who solved problems for world governments illegally. If something [covert] needed to be done, they called us. Morgan Brittany and Christopher Lloyd were in the pilot too. We had to rescue Elke Sommers, who played a starlet who had been kidnapped and held for ransom."

The pilot dearest to Seagren's heart was a special, hour-long episode of *Charlie's Angels* that was to have been the pilot for a spin-off series to be called *Toni's Boys*. "Barbara Stanwyck was to play the Bosley role from *Charlie's Angels*. We were three male angels," he said. It got great ratings when it aired as a *Charlie's Angels* episode. As a premise, it seemed to have "TiVo me" written all over it.

"I thought it was a can't-miss," said Seagren, a vaulting Valentino, but only a fallen "angel."

3 The Persistent Pupil

When it came to pole-vaulting, Brian Kelly and Mack could have been soul mates at Malone College. Kelly, however, had the soul of Peter Parker—after the radioactive spider bit him. At Malone College, Kelly would walk past the trophies displayed in niches in the wall in the foyer of Osborne Hall, the fieldhouse, and suddenly, he would become Spiderman. He would grab the sturdy brown frame around a display and hang there upside down. Mack, laughing, would seek one of the lesser-known exits for his getaway.

"It's a gift," Kelly said, modestly. "I was always the guy who kept Tim loose. It was like 'Stupid Human Tricks' on David Letterman."

They were best friends then. In fact, it was Kelly's development as a 17-foot jumper in 1992 that caught Mack's attention. They are best friends now. Mack trusts Kelly, an investments counselor, to attend to his financial portfolio. Today, palm-sized bronze plaques of Mack and Kelly hang on the wall in the gym lobby that Malone College reserves for its All-Americans.

Kelly, along with teammate Rich Hlaudy, whose plaque is also on the All-Americans' wall, recruited Mack to come to Malone, a member of the American Midwest Conference of the National Association of Intercollegiate Athletics (NAIA).

Mack went to the Quaker college because he felt pole-vault coach Ralph Schreiber, Kelly, and Hlaudy had a road map that could take him to the highway to heaven in the event. They didn't part ways until it became obvious that the sky was the limit for Mack, if not for them.

What times they had, jumping when the wind screamed and the sleet aligned itself in battle ranks behind that moaning bugle call, and only mad dogs and pole-vaulters were out. The pole vault is a difficult enough event anywhere. In the Great Lakes area, on the Malone football field, which is only a punt, pass, and kick from the Pro Football Hall of Fame in Canton, Ohio, and sits on a hill overlooking Interstate 77, it is daunting enough to make a man wish for superpowers. To jump in Ohio in the spring, you have to be efficient in temperatures only Mr. Freeze could love. The wind, a pole-vaulter's bane, is often fanged with sleet, which rattles off a man's skin like birdshot. Staying healthy is extremely hard.

At Malone, Schreiber was there every day they could practice, filming their jumps for step-by-step deconstruction later. Other times were high in a literal sense. There was no avoiding the initiation ritual, no ducking it for the men who rode the sticks. If you were a pole-vaulter, you clambered out on the rafters above the mats, maybe 30 feet high, with the monitors that the school's distance runners wore lashed to your chest, and your heart thumping like a jackhammer before you let go, and then you were falling into the pit of all your fears, screaming, shaking and alive in every cell of your body to have done it.

It wasn't the heights or the bravado that most drew Schreiber to Mack, however. It was a homelier quality. Kelly and Mark Croghan, who ran at Ohio State and became a two-time Olympian in the steeplechase, were teammates at Green High School in the Canton suburbs. Together, they took the small school to an Ohio state championship in track and field. Years later, it struck Schreiber, as Mack bloomed into a world-class pole-vaulter, that the sign that hung over the coach's door at Green High School really was a perfect description of Mack. It was a quote from, of all taciturn individuals, Calvin Coolidge, long before he became president of the United States.

"You always hear about Calvin Coolidge being 'Silent Cal,'" said Schreiber. "But he said at least one thing worth remembering. He said: 'Nothing in the world can take the place of persistence. Talent will not; nothing is more common than unsuccessful men with talent. Genius will not; unrewarded genius is almost a proverb. Education will not; the world is full of educated failures. Persistence and determination alone are omnipotent.'"

"That is as good a description as you are going to get of Tim Mack," Schreiber added. "He kept working and working, and he never gave up. He kept working and working, making small improvements until he got there."

He would jump 15–6 (4.70) his first year in college, 17–3 (5.26) the next year, on to 17–5 (5.31), then, after transferring to the University of Tennessee, 18–0½ (5.50) and 18–4½ (5.60) in his last season of eligibility. Mack said it was a long road, but it paid off. "I really just tried to get better at everything instead of just vaulting. Every year, I ran a little bit faster, lifted a little more weight, was more aware in the gymnastics room, threw the medicine ball farther, and did more gymnastics work. I never tried to be perfect, just better," he said.

The first forum in which he practiced his aggressive brand of self-improvement was the NAIA. It once turned out such players as the NBA's Scottie Pippen and Dennis Rodman as well as Major League Baseball's Brett Butler. But now television ignores it. The NAIA is not a branch of the National Collegiate Athletic Association. It has its own leagues and own national championships. The NAIA is simply another governing body for intercollegiate athletics in the United States. NAIA schools typically have less stringent academic requirements, but its members compete against NCAA schools in all divisions in most college sports. Malone pole-vaulters went over Notre Dame vaulters when they met them in meets during these years like airplanes go over your head.

Great athletes play in many different organizations. There were football players worthy of the NFL in the All-America Football Conference, the American Football League, the World Football League, and even the xecrable (CQ), xasperating (CQ) and quickly xtinct (CQ) XFL. There were great basketball players in the American Basketball Association, such as Julius "Dr. J" Erving. Wayne Gretzky began his hockey career in the World Hockey Association.

Likewise, there's no rule that great jumpers can only find their wings in the NCAA. In large part, the scholarship Schreiber gave Mack was serendipity. Schreiber worked as an official at track meets in the summer, prospecting for the kid whom the bigger schools had overlooked, the still-green pole-vaulter who would ripen later, the competitor who never surrendered, the guy whom Calvin Coolidge would have loved. He found him in Tim Mack.

"I first saw Tim jump at a Junior Olympics meet in Brunswick, Ohio, near Cleveland," Schreiber said. "I usually knew about the good vaulters in the area, but I didn't see him until after he graduated. He slipped under my radar. With his September birthday, he was very young for his class, so he had always been behind. He was tall, gangly, and his body was still developing. He had decent speed, so I thought he could be very good if he put on some weight and strength."

Like Mack's boyhood coaches before him, Schreiber quickly found that Mack could assemble the elements of the pole vault as quickly as Detroit put together automobiles. The Malone coach walked over to Mack, asked him his personal best, and passed on suggestions when he found it was 13-5¾ (4.11). "He cleared 14 feet [4.27] that day at that meet," Schreiber said. "Tim was willing to try anything you suggested."

Kelly and Hlaudy recruited for Malone College every time they cleared a bar. Now the Malone pole-vaulting coach had just met a young jumper who hadn't grown into his body yet, who came out of high school with no bad habits, and who soaked up coaching like a thirsty camel soaked up water at an oasis. Two more scouting trips to Mack's summer meets, and Schreiber was sold. So was Mack.

"It was easy to be impressed by Malone when you looked at Brian jumping 17-4 there. I thought that was unbelievable," said Mack.

"I didn't know if Tim was going to stay in the sport," Schreiber said. "He was going to go to the University of Toledo and walk-on [compete in hopes of earning a scholarship]. But they didn't have a strong program at the time."

Schreiber had pole-vaulted at Centre College in Kentucky. "I was way before fiberglass. In fact, I started with bamboo. Man, that thing was heavy. I used metal too, but I never got much over 9 feet," said Schreiber.

It would be tougher selling Mack's parents on Quaker Malone. The Macks are devout Catholics. Schreiber, however, had seen Kelly, a transfer from Ohio State, thrive at Malone, with its personalized attention and stricter rules. Kelly indisputably did not blossom until Malone, which has an enrollment of only 2,000, compared to Ohio State's nearly 50,000. "With some kids, it works out better to go to the small school first. I thought Tim could be one of those kids," Schreiber said.

On their official recruiting visit, the small college coach, who was gravity-bound in his day, and his two jumpers, who were clearing bars north of reality, deployed like commandos on a mission at the Macks' brick home in Westlake. Schreiber chatted easily with Mack, knowing he had already been convinced of Malone's vaulting virtuosity. Hlaudy, a devout Catholic, neutralized the doubts of Tim's mother about the school's religious orientation. Kelly talked sports with Tim's father and showed him Malone College's upcoming schedule. "When Tim's father looked at the schedule and asked Brian, 'Where do we go next?' I knew we had them," said Schreiber.

Kelly had occupied the room next to the dorm stairwell at Ohio State, and Flounder and the gang from *Animal House* seemed to go yelling up and down the steps at all hours of the night. Accordingly, he was frank with Mack when discussing the stricter rules of Malone.

"It's not like you have to become a Quaker, but Malone might not be the best place to be socially," Kelly said. "If you want to vault really high, though, you'll be able to do that."

This was not the "thee" and "thou" Quakerism of the movies. The Quakers believe in egalitarianism and brotherly love, in the Inner Light that illuminates each heart. They emphasize the conscientiousness with which a person pursues his calling.

Tim Mack had been conscientious about sports since he learned to ride a bike. His belief in himself was often the only bright spot in a career that could have been a snapshot of darkness. He subscribed to no one school of pole vaulting but borrowed what seemed helpful from anyone. He valued most of all his own internalized experiences as they translated into mathematical formulas that flamed like stars, guiding his path upward.

Much like St. Ignatius High School, Malone tries to instill a sense of ethical altruism. Its mission statement is posted inside a stairwell in Osborne Hall. The unobtrusive location seems to make it part of the everyday life of the school rather than putting it on ostentatious display in the foyer. "The mission of Malone College," it reads, "is to provide students with an education based on biblical faith in order to develop men and women of intellectual maturity, wisdom and Christian faith who are committed to serving the church, community and world."

As far as a party atmosphere goes, lamp shades were seldom used for millinery purposes at Malone College. Alcohol was not allowed anywhere on campus. Female visitors were allowed in men's dorm rooms three times a week—as long as the door to the room was open and both feet were on the floor.

"Tim lived next door, and I indirectly met my wife through Tim," said Kelly. "It was one of those opposite-sex nights in the dorm. Tim and I were guys who didn't exactly make our beds with painstaking care. Tim wasn't a slob, but he just had the sheets and covers pulled up over the pillows. My wife Ginger and another girl walked by, saw that, and started making the bed."

After seeing this, Kelly promptly raced from next door, piled into the bed like a kid making snow angels in fluffy powder, and started thrashing around with his arms and legs. Both feet were off the floor. Just this once.

"Although Tim and I were both raised Catholic, he didn't have that tough a time with it, because he had been to St. Ignatius," said Kelly.

Both liked nothing better than soaring to the rooftops of possibility. They would fool around after pole vault practice, dunking basketballs. Both could throw it down, although it had to be one of the stickier basketballs in the rack, and all their cylinders had to be firing. Still, practice was never a chore with them; it was fun up there where the air was fresh and sweet.

They also played on the same flag football team. "He was the quarterback, and I was the wide receiver," Mack said. "We were to the Malone flag football league what Peyton Manning and Marvin Harrison are to the NFL. We just knew where each other would be."

Tim was comfortable with his teammates and with Malone College. But to a pole-vaulter, a comfort zone can be where the danger zone begins.

A pole-vaulter often seems to be hanging right on the edge of crazy. The psychological demands are enormous. "It's a matter of just letting go and trusting your technique," Mack said. "To jump high, you almost have to put yourself in an unsafe position to get there."

Mack's hazing at Malone consisted of a rafter in Osborne Hall, a pole vault pit far below, and one scared daredevil never-be who would really rather be on the ground where things are nice and safe. "It's not that I have acrophobia," Mack said. "But I am not going to jump off a bridge, out of an airplane, or go cliff-diving anytime soon. I am not an extreme sports buff. I pole-vault."

As Mack inched his way above the floor, the heart monitor he was wearing reacted as a Geiger counter would have if the U.N. inspectors had actually found the WMD in Iraq. "Oh, we had a lot of fun with

Tim in the rafters," said Brian Kelly. "We had on the heart monitors the distance runners used to check their cardio fitness. We knew it bothered him. We could hear it chattering."

"I took it as a challenge. You had to do it, even though you're scared as can be, just to prove you're not a wimp," said Mack.

Hazing has gotten a very bad name in collegiate and interscholastic sports because of some gruesome excesses. It will never be stamped out, though, not in Olympic sports, which thrive on their identity as exclusive fraternities with demanding initiation rituals. Certainly it will not be extinguished in the pole vault, which skews to the extreme sports crowd anyway. "Pole-vaulters are the guys who would jump out of third-story fraternity windows into two inches of snow," said Ohio State athletic director Gene Smith.

For his part, Ralph Schreiber knew about the rafters ritual but preferred not to check too closely on it. Mack had to prove he would take a dare just like his other teammates had.

"The whole idea was to get him outside his comfort zone," Kelly said.

Mack passed the test, although his heart monitor might have hit full-tilt boogie when he was plummeting to the floor. "It sort of got you ready to pole-vault. When you're actually competing, you're too busy to worry about it," said Mack. "The pole vault happens so fast that you don't have time to think about being almost two stories off the ground. There's always something you're working on."

"Vaulters do crazy stuff," said Kelly. "Dave Volz [once ranked second in the U.S.] was at Indiana University at that time. He broke his ankle when he dropped from the rafters and missed the pole vault pit."

Volz invented a pole-vaulting move that came to bear his name, in which the vaulter steadied the bar with his hand as he tumbled over it. It was a miracle of touch and timing called "Volzing." The mental picture is of elegance, Strauss and the Vienna woods. Alas, they have played the last Volz.

Once the pegs were shortened, some Volzers went down six to eight inches overnight. Steadying the crossbar with the hand has now been specifically outlawed.

Pole-vaulting is a global village. When the Malone guys heard of a technique being used in France, they quickly adopted it. "We would throw a rope over the observation platform where they put cameras for basketball games," Kelly said. "Then we'd set up a pole vault pit and swing from the observation platform out over the bar on the rope. Again, anything out of your comfort zone helps."

"If you're going to vault 17–5 [the school record], as Tim eventually did at Malone, in the air upside down on a pole you have to understand your surroundings and know how to get out of trouble," Kelly said.

At Malone, Mack didn't win a NAIA championship, proof both of the quality of competition and of how far he had to go. "I think you have to look at whom he was competing against," said Kelly. "I was winning at Malone. Until Tim won an NCAA championship later in his career at Tennessee, he was always a step behind, even at Malone."

It didn't surprise Schreiber, however, that Mack became a two-time NAIA All-American at Malone. He had come to Malone as the nation's Junior Olympics champion. He had won the National Christian College Athletic Championship. "He always had the ability, and he was so coachable," Schreiber said.

The gold medal his old pupil had won in Athens didn't shock Schreiber either. "We talked about the Olympics from the very beginning. In the pole vault, you aim high," he said.

It was evident to Schreiber from the start that Mack had a technical strong point: his trail leg. Mack was red-shirted (kept from competing while reserving his year of eligibility) by injury his freshman year, because he developed a stress fracture in his left leg. A right-handed pole-vaulter like Mack takes off on his left leg, which then becomes the trail leg. This leg receives all the impact of the last step when the pole hits the back of the box. Theoretically, a vaulter tries to take off as the pole slams against the back of the box, reducing the stress. Theory, however, is not often practice. Most pole-vaulters overshoot their takeoff spot and are too close to the bar. A vaulter who is "under" at takeoff is slowing down and putting enormous stress on the back, groin and hamstring.

The worst year of Mack's career came in 1997, when he missed the entire season with a groin pull in his left leg. Later in his career, a calf injury canceled his indoor season after he won the gold medal.

The early stress fracture probably came from improper equipment and from overusing the takeoff leg and being under at takeoff. The groin pull was from the brutal demands made on the trail leg in the beginning stages of flight. The calf injury was probably associated with overuse, training at too high a peak too early in the season.

"His strength is his trail leg. He keeps it long and generates a whole lot of momentum to get himself upside down," said Schreiber. "His swing is very strong. He has been troubled by groin pulls because he stretched it when it was too tight. It's like a rubber band. You don't want to snap it by stretching it too far. But he had to be strong in everything to jump the heights he does."

In pole-vaulting, it's critical to keep the trail leg "long"—meaning only slightly bent. When Bubka vaulted, even when he was blasting to the box with more speed than any jumper ever possessed, the trail leg was a stilt. Full extension at takeoff begins with a long trail leg, so the pole-vaulter can execute a full swing. The trail leg in this instance acts like a lever. A shorter, bent lever (a tucked trail leg) does not generate as much momentum.

The same principle makes it advantageous for pole-vaulters to keep their arms straight on takeoff.

"People asked, 'How do you keep your trail leg so long?'" Mack said. "Well, it was the result of thousands of repetitions."

Typically, he devised a set of exercises he could use while laid up with the stress fracture. He would stand with a cut-down, short pole and go through the motions of jumping while just standing there. He would take the pole, put it over his head, and then bring it to his shoulders. Then, canting it upward and levering it down, he would pull it across his face and throw it away as if he were launched at long last. In his very first meet back, Mack cleared 15 feet. His previous career best had been 14–6.

Being a pole-vaulter, Mack also had a story behind the injury.

"We had a really short runway that was basically just a rubber mat rolled out across the gym floor," Mack said. "We also had these shoes that we thought were cool looking. They were high jump shoes, and the more I wore them, the more I felt pain in my shins. I'd ask the athletic department secretary for aspirin every day before practice. Eventually that got back to Ralph and he came to see me. I had developed a stress fracture from the shoes and the surface. "

High jump shoes are less flexible than pole vault shoes. Mack had grounded himself by seeking high style. "When he found out, Ralph was not very happy," Mack added.

Still, Schreiber had been more right about Mack than wrong. Strength came from the year-round training. Mack indeed had a big upside, and he improved rapidly as he grew stronger. "We started lifting in August. I wasn't used to lifting until later. We did pole-vault drills I wasn't doing until March," Mack said.

The environment also made him stronger mentally. "It's a big advantage in toughness being from the Midwest," he said. "I had to learn to jump in the snow, learn to jump when it was really cold."

Sometimes, athletes are disadvantaged by privilege. Mack was goaded by the absence of it.

Every day in an Ohio winter isn't a nice day. The surf isn't up. The surface of Lake Erie is frozen. If standards and a place to land were in place, Tim Mack and Brian Kelly would have practiced at Ice Station Zebra. "Even though I looked up to him at first, Brian was down to earth. He also really worked hard," Mack said. "He was one of those guys who never missed practice. I can count on the fingers of one hand the times I didn't go to practice myself."

"It sucked," Kelly said. "Snow would be on the runway. Ice would be in the box, and we had to chip it out. We would have our snowmobile mittens on, long Spandex pants, layers of clothes, jackets. We'd throw the jackets and mittens off then run down the runway and vault. We could at least stay warm by vaulting and running around, but Ralph couldn't."

The film study was part of it, too. It plays a huge role in the pole vault today in correcting more serious flaws as well as slight technical glitches.

Tim would come to think of his tactics as his greatest strength. "To be a good pole-vaulter, you have to be a student of the event," said Kelly. "Even if somebody is telling you something that you know is wrong, listen to him. You might be able to apply it in a different way to yourself."

If things had turned out differently, Kelly might have had the big career, not Mack. His coach knew how good he was. "Brian got married, and the kids started coming along," Schreiber said. "But it gets in their blood. Brian is still competing. He has mats in his backyard. He sells poles."

In 2003 Kelly won the open pole vault competition at Ohio State's Jesse Owens Classic, adapting on the fly, using every trick he learned on the wind-blown, frost-flecked runways of his past. "There must have been a 20-mile-per-hour crosswind blowing," he said. "I compensated by starting two feet off the runway and letting it blow me onto it."

You could also see the Ohio State kids wondering what in the name of galloping senility Kelly was up to. "I'm sure they thought, 'What's this old fart doing?'" Kelly said. "Well, getting over a bar is what he was doing. My last jump was my best jump, and I won because I was the only one to clear a bar."

By the end, one of the Buckeyes' vaulters was starting on the side too, playing the wind. He almost made it.

Nothing matters but setting the bar higher. By the time he left Malone, Tim Mack was riding the bent pole ever higher, heading for the other end of the rainbow.

Slightly more than a mile from the entrance of Malone College, the football-shaped roof of the Pro Football Hall of Fame juts into the sky like the kickoff of a game not even NFL Films can blow out of proportion. From pro football's crude pioneers to the stars of, seemingly, only a few minutes ago, the NFL scrupulously honors its legends. It isn't like that at Malone College. Today, the weathered yellow brick of Osborne Hall has little to indicate that an Olympic gold medalist once learned his trade inside it. The All-American plaque and his name on a list of school records are the only mentions of his name. The school displayed stories about Mack's victory in Athens for a time but later removed them.

Most schools love for their name to be mentioned by the media, unless it's in connection with the word "violations." But in the gym, none of the twenty-four banners and signs commemorating Malone's success mentions Mack. Of course, he didn't graduate from the school. Still, he has to be the greatest name ever to have walked its hallways and certainly the greatest to have used its gym.

Mack headed south to SEC track power: the University of Tennessee. He resisted talk of Signs From Above when he was leaving Malone after three years (counting the red-shirt year) and heading to Tennessee. He called it simply a "gut feeling." "Ralph thought it was a smart move for me to move on to a higher level and so did Brian," said Mack, who diligently began writing NCAA Division I schools.

He sent fifteen to twenty letters out, and the Volunteers were the first to get back to him. Schreiber knew Vols pole vault coach Jim Bemiller well from the Ohio high school ranks. Bemiller was a vaulter at Miami University and a native of Mansfield in central Ohio. He thought "B"—as Bemiller had been known since his days of wearing a single-initialed letter jacket in high school—and Mack would be a good match. It takes a high level of altruism for a coach to send an NAIA All-American elsewhere at an obvious cost to his own program.

"But Ralph knew Bemiller had some good pole-vaulters and knew what he was doing," Kelly said. "Ralph might not always say the politically correct thing for a coach, and he might not always do the best thing for the school, but for the athletes, he was great. For Tim to have gone to Malone was absolutely the right choice. Ralph might not be the best coach, but nobody cares more than Ralph."

A matter-of-fact Schreiber said his prize pupil needed to vault year-round, which was clearly impossible in Ohio. Schreiber also noted that Mack had outgrown Malone's facilities. The bleachers, with those easily accessible rafters, were near the Osborne Hall pole vault pit. Mack often saw them out of the corner of his eye as he practiced. He also saw the huge air-conditioning units that hang just below the roof in each corner of the gym. When the sunlight poured through the windows at the end of the gym, a vaulter on that short runway could see only sky and the rumbling vents, only promise and menace. "I never got as close to them as Brian Kelly, but I always worried about hitting them," Mack said.

"About 18 feet or so was the most they could clear in there," Schreiber said. "There just wasn't a lot of room. But we would fool around and set the bar at the world record, and they each would take three jumps at it. They got to where they could kick it off."

When Mack visited Tennessee, it was midsummer, and next to nobody was on campus. "I knew I was going there, just like I knew I was going to Malone," Mack said. "I left a lot of friends, but, just like at Malone, I got into another good group with some more terrific friends."

Mack and Kelly were driving back from the Earl Bell meet in Arkansas before Tim transferred to Tennessee in 1993, leaving on a Saturday, one day early, because Tim had to be on campus in Knoxville by Monday. "The song 'Pray for Me' by Michael W. Smith came on the radio, as we were driving back to Malone," Kelly said. "Tim and I liked to sing along. But the lyrics really hit us that day."

Although not a big Christian music fan, Mack was singing a song that became the next part of his life story. The song is about new starts, using a fork in the road as its metaphor. Mack would take, literally and figuratively, the highway.

"I was already going to Tennessee, so I don't know if I considered the song a sign," said Mack. "But it was definitely one of those gut feelings."

It's a song about the love of friends and God's love. It's about memories, like the Stupid Human Tricks, the ride down from the rafters, the dunks, the laughter, the bonding. It is about making new memories. It's about letting go and exploring.

Again, Mack was about to go outside the comfort zone.

❨4❩ Danger

The flowers come every year in February. Ed Dare is grateful February is the shortest month. He couldn't stand any more of it.

The Dare house sits in a development in Port Matilda in central Pennsylvania that you reach by a two-lane road that twists and turns around the flank of the Appalachians. The wooded foothills were snow-covered on the last weekend in February 2005, and the sun was playing peek-a-boo with the clouds. Winter doesn't let go easily in Port Matilda—located just a slalom run from State College, the home of Penn State University—especially in February.

Ed Dare sat in the den of his two-story brick home, surrounded by mementos of what he had lost. "This is a tough week. This week was three years," he said. "It's always a tough week. The whole kitchen is solid flowers. So many people from around the country remember Kevin, remember that day three years ago."

On February 23, 2002, in the Big Ten Indoor Track and Field Championships in Minneapolis, Kevin Dare became possibly the most accomplished pole-vaulter ever to die in the event. He was nineteen years old. Making his first jump at 15 feet, 7 inches (4.75)—a height that seemed to pose no problem, for he had cleared 17 feet two weeks before the meet in practice—Dare went up, but his forward momentum stopped at the peak of his jump. He came down on the wrong side of the bar, slamming his unprotected head against the steel vault box.

"I didn't like to talk to him before a meet," said Ed. "But I'll never forget what he said to me: 'Dad, this is going to be my day.'"

Kevin, a Penn State sophomore, had the fifth-best jump in the Big Ten his sophomore season, and he thought he could medal in the conference meet.

"Everything looked good," said his father, who had helped coach him for the six years Kevin had pole-vaulted. "The plant was good, but he was a little under [too close to the box] on the takeoff. The invert was good. But the pole shot him straight up. I've heard so many stories about what happened. I've heard he landed headfirst. Well, he landed on his back, half in the pads and half in the box."

Pole-vaulters, in the top-gun slang that characterizes their world, call it "stalling out." It can be caused by poor takeoff or by gripping the pole too high.

Ed and his wife Terri always went to Kevin's meets. First to last.

"I was down there before the paramedics, and I saw the blood. That's when I knew he was in trouble," Dare said.

Medical personnel tried to pull the parents away. Dare remembers hearing someone say, "He's his father," and then they let him through. Track officials kept Terri Dare from getting close enough to see.

"I never left his side," Ed said.

The dry language of the autopsy describes a massive wound and determined the cause of death being head injuries caused by a fall from height. Ed made a wish, like a man who had seen a falling star. "I know I can't bring Kevin back, but I don't want another pole-vaulter or another family to go through what we went through," he said. "When I talk to people in pole vaulting, I say, 'Take advantage of me. I have been through this. I know what hell is like.'"

If the Dares had their way, it would be the day that changed the pole vault. Ed Dare calls himself the "Ralph Nader" of the sport, after the consumer advocate. He has nothing at stake but safety, he said, no position in the sport, no endorsements. As a direct result of his emotional crusade for safety measures, the landing pit is now bigger. The optimum landing area is painted on the pads, so the jumpers have a target. There is a "soft box," padded by space-age shock absorption material, which largely came to be manufactured for the sport on Dare's initiative. The base of the standards is now padded. Dare said, when he first tried to do that, he had to use pads taken from volleyball standards. No one in track and field manufactured them for the pole vault.

From 1983 to 1997, thirteen high school pole-vaulters died and seven others incurred catastrophic injuries. Two high school pole-vaulters and Kevin Dare died in 2002. In April 2008, high school pole-vaulter Ryan Moberg died after striking the box with his unprotected head in Walla Walla, Washington. In March 2005, a Penn State pole-vaulter broke his arm. In the World Championships in Helsinki in the summer of 2005, Finnish vaulter Matti Mononen snapped off a part of the measuring equipment on one of his misses during qualifying. Later in the prelim, Chinese pole-vaulter Liu Feiliang landed on a plastic chair by the side of the track, breaking one of his legs. As ever, it is dangerous up there.

But the pole vault has been dangerous since it was invented. So has training for it. Brian Sternberg of the University of Washington owned the world record at 16–8 (5.08 meters) in 1963 in the infancy of the fiberglass pole. He was twenty years old. An All-American gymnast, Sternberg fell headfirst while doing trampoline exercises and broke his neck. The permanent paralysis that resulted made Sternberg, who many considered to have a chance to clear 17 feet and perhaps far beyond, the sport's lost boy—its biggest example of what might have been.

Even today, there are virtually no pole vault–specific helmets in use, although they are on the market now at a cost of slightly less than $100 each. The Ralph Nader of the sport thinks that the lack of a helmet makes pole-vaulting unsafe at any height.

"All I hear are two things: A helmet might impede progress, and it might give them a false sense of security and cause them to be more aggressive," Dare said. "Vaulters also worried that if they set a world record, it wouldn't be recognized [because of the soft box]. But Sergey Bubka himself was in charge of testing the soft box. The IAAF now certifies it."

By 2008, six states mandated helmets for high school jumpers; Washington state was not one of them. Minnesota did so only weeks after Kevin Dare's death. The national pole vault safety governing body has yet to certify any helmet. "The same old fraternity, the good old boy network of about fifteen people, runs pole vaulting in the United States," Dare said.

The pole vault is the most dangerous school sport in America. It has had more catastrophic (fatal or permanently disabling) injuries, per capita, than any sport, including football. An estimated 25,000 high school athletes pole-vault. Over 90,000 athletes are involved at all ages. It is an X Game in spikes. The heights are so much greater than in the high jump, the other vertical jump, that the pole vault could be called track and field's Gravity Game. The pole, even after a successful vault, can travel under the crossbar and strike pole-vaulters in the armpit, the face, or the shorts. "I have seen some big-time scars," said Jim Bemiller.

"If I had the chance to turn back the clock, I would do it totally different," Ed Dare said. "No one disclosed to us how dangerous it is."

"We never thought of it as a type of extreme sport," said Terri Dare. "It's not mountain climbing. It's not stepping in front of a bus. People are supposed to get up. People are supposed to survive."

The pole vault attracts the young and can encourage the reckless. They get out on the edge, where they unfasten the tethers of caution and fear, and they can flame out like Icarus. It is simply not a buckle-your-seatbelts sport. Stacy Dragila, the first female to win an Olympic gold medal in the pole vault, goes to her workouts each day with the cryptic motto "5MODT" written on her training sheet. It means "Five Meters [16–4¾] Or Die Trying."

"I understand her thinking," Ed Dare said. "My son died at the Big Ten Indoors. In those circumstances, you're maxed up. It's a violent sport. They have a responsibility to make it as safe as possible."

Said Bob Fraley, the coach at Fresno State, as well as the coordinator of the pole vault for USA Track and Field: "The element of risk is what people love in our sports culture. It is why NASCAR has gone out of sight. But that might have to change."

"We relish the daredevil image and reckless behavior. But we really can't. This event won't allow you to do that," said Greg Hull, the coach of 2000 Olympic gold medalist Nick Hysong.

"There is a neglect factor," said Bemiller. "We have short [track] seasons in the Midwest. Few high school coaches have actually vaulted. Put that combination together and kids are thrown out there to compete too soon."

The pole vault is also a very expensive sport. This can lead struggling school districts to scrimp on equipment. World-class poles cost $500 each. Landing pits can be an enormous investment, running well over $10,000. They must be scrupulously maintained.

"The successful vaulters often get their fathers involved. You need good equipment. Good poles are expensive. You need good coaching. It sort of skews to high school districts with a strong middle-class base," said Bemiller.

The development of synthetic fibers to be used in poles in the 1970s took the event to new heights, for all that it also led to the regrettable creation of polyester leisure suits. With greater heights came greater risks. But "Stayin' Alive" was not supposed to be about the pole vault.

There are several components to a successful pole vault. The Dares and pole vault officials differ on what happened on many of them at the 2002 Big Ten Indoor Championships.

Practice: Rules changes have outlawed "tapping" at all levels. When a pole-vaulter taps, it means another competitor or a coach gives a boost to a pole-vaulter in practice. Usually, it is in the form of a push in the back as the vaulter nears the box to increase speed. It creates a false sense of ability.

Ed Dare is adamant that Kevin was not "getting a tap" in Minneapolis. However, Jan Johnson, bronze medalist in the 1972 Olympics and chairman of the committee of pole vault safety in the USA since 1994, said, "I have at least ten witnesses that Kevin Dare was tapping that day. They say he was jumping well and penetrating deep into the pits. Well, yeah. With a tap." Johnson decried an "epidemic" of tapping in American colleges and universities before Dare was killed.

Size of Pole: Poles are calibrated for a competitor's weight. Using one not designed to carry a competitor's body weight is illegal for high school and AAU pole-vaulters. Johnson wants to make it illegal at all levels. The rule has curtailed many of the injuries that once resulted from snapping poles and the deadly shrapnel they created. "It is like a concussion grenade going off in your hands, like the mother of all fastballs on your fists on a cold day," said Tim Mack, who has only broken one pole.

Pole-vaulters learn to somersault into the landing pit when a pole snaps. Toby Stevenson, Mack's top rival in 2004, safely "ejected" from a shattered pole in such a manner in 2005.

"I think it all goes back to mental approach," said Hull. "Young kids in college and high school think, 'if I just try harder, if I just get on a bigger pole, I can please coach or please dad.' You have to look at it and realize it demands a certain respect and attention."

Grip: A higher grip means more leverage for a higher arc on the jump. It also can result in a shallower jump. A lower grip allows for deeper penetration into the pit. High school pole-vaulters can't grip higher than pole manufacturers' specifications. The only prohibition in the NCAA, USA Track and Field, and IAAF is that the pole-vaulter may not move the upper hand or raise the lower hand above the upper during the vault.

"Kevin Dare was holding too high on the pole, which caused his accident," said Jan Johnson. "That caused him to get pushed on his back and not reach the pit."

Kevin's father, perhaps predictably in the charge/countercharge that has flared between the family and pole vault officials, said his son had been on that pole with that grip before.

Coaching: Kevin Dare's vaulting coach, Tom Kleban, was confined to a wheelchair as a result of a teenage swimming accident. He was not with him in Minneapolis. That is not unusual in pole-vaulting. To a dismaying degree in such a dangerous sport, the pole-vaulters almost coach themselves.

Sergey Bubka advocates sound coaching over any other measures. "I would focus on coaching," he said. "If you have good coaching, then there is no problem at all. It goes to the quality of the coaches and to learning proper techniques."

Standards: Reports from Minneapolis said Kevin had set the standards close to the box, at 35 centimeters (1 foot, 1¾ inches), leaving very little margin for error between the box and the bar. New NCAA rules following Kevin's death mandated that the standards not be closer than 45 centimeters (about 1–5¾). The NCAA and AAU use a 40-centimeter (1–3¾) minimum. There is no minimum setting in USATF and IAAF competitions. According to rules official Stanley Underwood: "Equipment permitting, the bar could be set directly over the top of the back of the plant box!"

Tim Mack never sets them nearer the box than 50 centimeters (1–7¾). By international track rules, they can be shifted from 30 centimeters (11¾ inches) to 80 centimeters (1–11½).

"The comments about Kevin setting the standards have been all over the place. Kevin's roommate and fellow vaulter said they were at his normal settings," said Ed Dare.

In news reports the day after Kevin's death, Ed was quoted as saying 35 centimeters was close to Kevin's usual position and that the setting did not contribute to his death.

Experience: Pole-vaulters between the ages of nineteen and twenty-one, college freshmen and sophomores, suffer the most catastrophic injuries. About 30 percent of all attempts are aborted in the Olympics, according to Greg Hull. He cites the figure as a tribute to the experience of the Olympians. He believes this shows they are savvy enough to bail out when they know the jump is unsafe. But in the 2004 men's Olympic final, the very highest level of pole-vaulting in the world, Russia's Pavel Gerasimov withdrew after taking off on the far right side of the runway, knocking off the bar at 18 feet, 6½ inches (5.65), and then landing flat on his back on the infield, missing the pit. In the women's Olympic pole vault qualifying, Russia's Anastasiya Ivanova landed awkwardly in the pits and broke her leg on a jump of 14–5¼ (4.40).

"Tim Mack has a notebook with him for a reason," said Fraley, referring to the game plan Mack devised over many years that takes into account varying conditions, sizes of poles, and heights. "Tim looks at what he did the last two years, and then he takes the environment at the meet into consideration. A lot of people go out there with preconceived ideas of what pole they will be on at what height. But what if it's raining? What if there's a headwind? You've got to make adjustments."

Ed Dare said his son was an analytical jumper. Others thought he was barely in control, according to Jan Johnson.

"There was only one Olympic-caliber athlete who was a free spirit and changed, only one associated with the pole vault—Toby Stevenson," said Hull.

Stevenson seriously injured himself in Oslo in 2002 and was in the hospital for two weeks with a punctured lung.

"It is ballet but with violent impact. If you're not careful, the pole vault will chew you up and spit you out," said Bemiller.

According to a study by the Center for Catastrophic Sports Injuries at the University of North Carolina, the vast majority of fatalities and catastrophic injuries have resulted from landing behind or outside the pit.

The proposed safety measures have drawn mixed reviews.

Bigger Pits: The larger pits are universally applauded. Pole vault pits now should be no smaller than six meters (19–8¼) wide by five meters (16–4¾) long behind the box with front pads of two meters (6–6¾) extending to the front of the box. "We interviewed the people involved in catastrophic injuries from 1972 on, forty-seven cases," said Johnson. "It took five years to run them all down. A lot of school districts wanted to wait until they got the proof before enlarging the pits."

The Soft Box: "I've seen jumps off the soft box, and they're great," Bob Fraley said. "There's nothing wrong with it. But it's close to $2,000 for a soft box, and there are substantial other changes. You have to tear up the runway and tear out the old box, pour new concrete, and put rubber strips down to pad it. And it's not just one box. It's three or four in some places. If you're building a new facility, by all means consider the soft box. For an older facility, it's a huge amount of money." Penn State was the first customer for the soft box.

For as little as $150, however, a box collar that uses the same force absorption technology can be fitted around the steel box.

"They've padded everything that can be padded. I think it has had a clear effect on reducing injuries," said Bemiller.

Helmets: Dare rummaged in a cupboard and brought out a shiny black helmet. It is astonishingly lightweight at just over one pound (500 grams). The helmet has cutouts on the sides so as not to impede the pole-vaulter's arms when he is planting the pole for takeoff. It is thinner over the forehead than at the rear. "No one lands on his forehead in the pole vault," said Ed Dare. According to Dare, 97 percent of catastrophic injuries occur to the rear of the head.

The helmet was developed by a company called Enventys. Each helmet bears a small logo on its back, a white outline of a pole-vaulter planting a bending pole and lifting one foot off the ground, ready to fly. It's the pole vault's equivalent of the Michael Jordan symbol, in which "Air Jordan" is captured just after takeoff, legs scissored, the ball held like a cocked gun in one hand. The figure on the pole-vaulting helmet is modeled on a photograph of Kevin Dare in competition.

The helmet uses the same shock-absorption technology that a company named Skydex has patented for many applications, including playground equipment for children and boats used by the Navy SEALs. Tests show the cushioning technology makes a dramatic difference in absorption of force in comparison to naked steel boxes.

From as slight a distance as six inches, a pole-vaulter could die from his head hitting a steel box. It would take a fall of over 18 feet to generate such lethal force on a soft box.

In 2007 a pole-vaulting helmet was approved by the American Society of Testing and Materials but has not been mass-produced.

"The day Kevin died, we heard from three pole-vaulters who said they were quitting the sport," Ed Dare said. "The pole-vaulting community wanted to say, 'Golly, what a shame' and then go on about life as before. Basically, without the national high school federations adopting the helmet, we won't be safe at the learning level."

"I'm not convinced," said Fraley. "I'm concerned with flexion. What if a helmet on the head hits the pads and puts more torque on the neck?"

"I would rather be efficient and safe in my technique than use a helmet," said Mack.

"If you pole-vault a long enough time, you will over-rotate and hit the pit more on your head and shoulders than on your hind end and back," said Jan Johnson. "That happened three times to me. When that happens, your head gets pushed toward your chest, and it stretches the back of your neck a little bit. I question whether a helmet that adds 1 to 1½ more inches to the back of the neck wouldn't create more leverage."

"It's a cop-out," Dare said. "The people who run pole vaulting are bull shitters. Jan Johnson is a bull shitter. You can quote me on it. I call him the 'Chameleon.' One day, he's for safety. The next day, he's not."

Then Ed Dare said: "Jan Johnson has a daughter who pole-vaults, and she doesn't even wear a helmet," he said.

Jan's daughter, Chelsea Johnson, who holds the NCAA women's record, does not wear a helmet because her father gave her that option.

Bob Richards, the two-time Olympic gold medalist, supports helmets. But they are damned in the eyes of young competitors for lack of cool.

"When I asked Kevin about using one, he told me Jeff Hartwig [the American record-holder] and the elite guys don't wear one. And coaches don't have the guts to mandate it," said Ed Dare.

The argument that helmets are dorky is a weak one. As soon as the best player in ice hockey, Wayne Gretzky, put on a helmet a generation ago, the "cool" issue in that sport was resolved. Yet of all the elite pole-vaulters in the world, only Toby Stevenson wears a protective helmet. He did so when he began vaulting as a boy to soothe his mother's fears.

The flimsy roller hockey helmet he wears was never designed for the stresses of pole-vaulting, though. In 2007 the American Society of Testing and Materials approved a pole vault–specific helmet. No manufacturer has yet come forward to produce them to ASTM specifications.

The inescapable fact is that a mistake in the pole vault can be very costly. It is like what journeyman heavyweight boxer Randall "Tex" Cobb once said of his bloody craft: "If you make a mistake in tennis, it's love-15. If you make a mistake in boxing, it's your ass, darlin'."

How does most of the pole-vaulting community see the accident that killed Kevin Dare—a freakish occurrence? Neglect of safety? Disorientation?

"The pole vault community looks on it as pilot error," Fraley said.

Ed Dare considered suing. His attorney, Rob Sachs, advised against it. In his heart, Sachs felt extra protection would make pole-vaulters extra reckless. "It would make it a faster, harder, rougher sport, as has happened in hockey," he said.

It is a feeling shared by Chico Kyle, Tim Mack's high school coach. "It [a helmet] sort of leads them to think they're invulnerable," said Kyle.

Of the possibility for serious injury, he said: "It's always in the back of your mind."

Bemiller, Mack's coach at Tennessee and afterward, thinks the problem is the increasing popularity of the pole vault in the extreme sports culture.

"The pole vault is not for everyone," said Bemiller. "It takes a good overall athlete to handle the event, let alone compete well. The vaulter used to be one of the best overall athletes on the track team—good hurdler, good relay man, long jumper. Now it has become an attraction for the below-average athlete who likes the 'trick' side of the event. The kids need to know this is an intense thing. I tell the young college kids that there are no half-speed pole-vaults. You have to be in shape and focused enough to come down that runway full speed for twelve to fifteen times at practice, all out. I tell them it's like tackling a running back in football. You better hit that guy like Ray Lewis or Dick Butkus, or he will run all over you. Be in shape and know what you are doing in the pole vault."

Pole vault officials look nervously over their shoulders at the Dare family. "This whole issue is a political hot-potato," said one internationally known pole vault coach. "That father could sue and bury us if he wanted to."

Ed Dare smiled bleakly. He is used to being painted as a zealot, a crusader, a man out to save pole-vaulting by destroying it. It is, he said, a distortion.

Terri Dare stood near his desk, wiping her eyes with Kleenex and sobbing softly. To her side was a picture of Eric, their older son. Next to it was one of Kevin. On the opposite wall, framed, was a Penn State track singlet in dark blue and white, as simple and unadorned as the uniforms of Joe Paterno's football team.

"I've heard that I'm against pole-vaulting and that economic reasons and insurance could mean the end of the event. Why would I try to put the pole vault out of commission?" said Dare. "Kevin loved pole-vaulting. He would haunt me every day if I did that."

This argument often boils down to dry statistics, to impact velocity in tests, to arguments over the thickness of the back of the new helmet and its effect in possibly hyper-extending pole-vaulters' necks. But to see what is at stake in the safety debate, you have to move beyond the numbers. You have to drive the road in central Pennsylvania that hugs the hills, to the house with the funeral parlor of a kitchen. To give an abstract debate a human face, you would have had to meet Kevin Dare, who was always smiling.

In the slightly esoteric sport of pole vaulting, at a place like Penn State, where there is football and then there is everything else, Kevin Dare was George Bailey of *It's a Wonderful Life.* He touched so many people's lives. The place would have been immeasurably poorer without him. Kevin didn't need a lot for his ego and never was really into himself. His pickup truck, his country music, the track uniform he wore when he went through the launch window on a spindly pole—they mattered. So did people, all kinds of people.

"He was always for the underdog," Ed said. "Always."

He was the reigning U.S. national junior champion in 2002. A fierce competitor, he had won a memorable storm-tossed, weather-beaten high school state championship just two years earlier for State College Area High School. That day at Shippensburg State, the boys were pole-vaulting in a downpour, Ed will tell you in exasperation. Kevin almost no-heighted his first bar in the crossfire of wind and rain, but officials wouldn't move the event inside. "It was a monsoon, but they said some of the jumpers only had shoes for outside. So let's continue when it's unsafe," Dare said.

Kevin managed to squeeze the best jump of the day between the raindrops. In a framed photograph that rests on a shelf behind his father's desk, Kevin stands on the highest point of the victory podium, flanked by the rivals over whom he had flown. Umbrellas bloom in the hands of the spectators standing behind them like mushrooms sprouting in a marshy field. The bronze medalist was Kevin's great friend and rival, Dave Bollinger, who went on to vault at Penn State.

"Dave fell in the box that day and was hurt too badly to continue vaulting. He still finished third," Ed Dare said.

It was Bollinger who arranged for the Nittany Lion singlet to be given to the Dare family.

In sports, everything is quantified. Box scores in baseball and basketball are dense with figures. In track, every footrace is timed down to the runners' reaction time to the starter's pistol. In the field events, the jumps and the throws, every effort is scrupulously measured down to the last centimeter. Adversity is usually the template sports applies. How does an athlete perform when up against it? How does he cope when the weather is mean and surly enough to be slashing the Lake Erie shoreline in Cleveland? But it was the quality of humility that was the measure of Kevin Dare.

As a pole-vaulter, his mission was to rise above hard times. As a country music fan, one of his favorite songs was Toby Keith's "What Do You Think of Me Now?" The remarkable thing about his death is that the loss touched so many people from all walks of college and high school life. They all thought so highly of him. Jocks and nerds are usually segregated as completely as if there were some system of apartheid in effect, one based on muscle fibers and barbells. Kevin Dare was a good ol' boy, but he was comfortable outside the circle of team and family. He always included outsiders.

"When he was a little boy, he literally would not let us kill a caterpillar," Ed said. "He made us pick it up off the sidewalk."

"I don't think he even wanted us to kill flies," said Terri Dare.

In some ways, counting team managers as friends and easing the way for lowly freshmen when he was a senior football captain in high school made him as defiant of conventions as his daredevil brethren. Jumping off high places is something of a tradition in the pole vault. But when you land, you walk the same ground everyone else does.

Kevin didn't think the big air inflated him into someone bigger than life. Kevin Dare saw every caterpillar as a butterfly in the making. He once studied with another student until 3:30 in the morning, even though he didn't take the class, trying to ensure she didn't fail. He made sure to include little brothers and friends of friends in his conversations. He gave rides in the pickup truck to the manager of the State College Area High football team. "He was always there when you needed him, like a knight in shining armor. His armor was his old brown Ford pickup, and his blade was his pole, and that's how I'll always remember him," wrote Kun R. Anderson, State College High, Class of 2001, on an Internet tribute page to Kevin.

Kevin gave polite compliments to economically deprived kids who didn't have the money for the latest clothes. He shared a headset with a friend, each with one headphone pressed to his ear, the two arm-in-arm, laughing and dancing in the aisle of the bus on the way to Lehigh University and an indoor meet.

Perhaps the most affecting comments came from a rival, Brian Mondschein, a Hershey, Pennsylvania, pole-vaulter who won the state indoor and outdoor championships a year after Dare had won it. Mondschein became a three-time All-American and NCAA outdoor runner-up as a vaulter at Virginia Tech. He religiously kept tabs on Dare's marks in high school and exultantly told his parents the day he jumped five meters (16–4¾): "I finally caught up with him!"

It was February 23, 2002.

"When I found out what happened, I couldn't believe it," Mondschein wrote. "He loved it so much, and it killed him. He was definitely a role model. He was the top vaulter in Pennsylvania. I was always chasing his marks. Yet he always had time to talk to you."

Mondschein's father, a former pole-vaulter, started him in the event when he was 14. His grandfather, Irving "Moon" Mondschein, finished eighth in the 1948 Olympic decathlon. Despite such a rich athletic background, Brian Mondschein red-shirted in the outdoor season following Kevin Dare's death.

"I was spooked," he said. "I couldn't get his death out of the back of my mind."

He remembered a Rutgers pole-vaulter who landed on the box on his back and broke his hip. He remembered a Southern Illinois vaulter, Ray Scotten, who was knocked unconscious at the 2004 NCAA Championships. Scotten tripped in his final steps of the approach. He bent the pole as he stumbled, and the fiberglass slingshot fired him to the left of the pit, where he sailed over a six-foot-high fence and landed in the stands. He remembered Kevin Dare.

It's dangerous up there, yet Mondschein resumed vaulting the next season. On the runway, he wears only the same style of skateboarding helmet he used as a beginner. "I feel comfortable in it," said Mondschein.

In meets across the Big East Conference and in the NCAA Championships, Mondschein said he has never seen a soft box. "The area where Kevin fell in the box is still as hard as ever," he said.

Kevin Dare was a respected name in "Happy Valley," as the students call Penn State. It is "The Land That Time Forgot" in many ways. Joe Paterno has been on the football staff since 1950. He has been the head coach since 1966. He seems to have run the same predictable offense forever. Nothing seems to change there. But Kevin changed his fellow students' hearts and minds.

"Be sure to go to the student bookstore," Terri Dare said. "They did such a wonderful job."

At the corner of College Ave. and Hiester St., across the street from the Penn State campus, a vast mural called *Inspiration* decorates an entire outside wall of the store. A local artist named Terry Pilato painted it and dedicated it to those who touched the lives of other people in Centre County, Pennsylvania. Painted just behind Jerry Sandusky, the long-time Penn State offensive coordinator in football, and near the great icon of Paterno himself is Kevin Dare. His pet ferret "Gizzy" (for "Gizmo"), which he smuggled into and out of his dorm room his entire freshman year, is perched on his shoulder. A gold medal dangles around his neck. On the mural, Kevin is blond-haired, 19 forever, eternally smiling, with a halo shining around his head.

"Kevin had an inspirational sign that read: 'Your talent is God's gift to you; what you do with it is your gift back to God,'" said Ed Dare. "So many times I've wanted to quit. Then I remember the caterpillar. Kevin was caring every day of his life."

"I've been blessed with some wherewithal and some organizational ability," he continued. "So I set up a foundation. I'm trying to get this to be self-sustaining so track programs can afford soft boxes and helmets."

He hopes to make the Kevin J. Dare Foundation his martyred son's legacy to the sport. A bittersweet smile flickered across Ed Dare's face like the sun moving between the clouds on the icy day outside his window. "The IRS loves foundations," Dare said, sarcastically. "I haven't made any money on any of this. This has cost me money."

He said he doesn't understand the delays. "NASCAR had head restraints the season after Dale Earnhardt died," he said. "The NHL put up its first nets sixty-five days after the young girl [thirteen-year-old Brittanie Cecil] was killed by a puck."

Actually, it was the next season in the NHL.

But this is a black-and-white matter to Ed Dare. Right and wrong stand in as stark contrast as the colors of the pole vault helmet.

"I think ever since his son died, Ed Dare has tried to make everything right in pole vaulting. I think he really loved his son," Jan Johnson said. "He's done a little bit that's good and a little bit that's unwise. I think he has too much faith that the answers are the soft box and helmets."

The pole vault community has stepped up its educational programming since Kevin Dare's death. College coaches attend a pole-vault safety clinic before each season. Jan Johnson, noting his daughter's online driver education class years ago, offers an online class. He has gone from one coach per day registering for it in 2003 to fifteen a day in 2005. It continues to grow.

Many in pole vaulting think Kevin Dare's death accelerated the pace of rule changes to make the sport safer. But Ed Dare is a human searchlight. Until the standards quit looking like a gallows to him, until helmets are mandatory, he won't be satisfied.

"The NHL and NASCAR were in the public eye, that's why they changed," he said. "In pole vaulting, it's been six years now, and there haven't been any more fatalities. Nothing is going to change until the first woman pole-vaulter dies. Then there is going to be an outcry like you won't believe."

The influx of women competitors has been crucial in pole vaulting. Even before the tragedies mounted at the start of the new century, the sport was often a victim of budget cuts. It was costly. It was not egalitarian, but instead skewed to rich districts. But pole vaulting would never be cut once it became a gender equity issue. In many ways, it has been saved by the very people who were thought to be too weak, and perhaps too susceptible to the vapors at the height of a jump, to do it.

The outcry Dare feared almost happened in 2001. Kelsey Koty, a female pole-vaulter at Eastern Washington University, veered to the right on her first jump as a collegian, hitting the bar and then the side of the pit. The pit was not compliant with specifications instituted after Kevin Dare's death. She bounced off the pit and struck her head on the floor of the EWU field house. She was in a coma after suffering injuries that included an epidural hemorrhage, loss of smell, impairment of speech, and cognitive dysfunction. She spent three weeks in intensive care. She had two metal plates inserted into the back of her head where her skull had been fractured. Koty even had to learn to walk again. She never pole-vaulted again, although she did compete later as a long jumper.

Dare's comment about a female fatality recalled her tragedy on the other side of the country while he still wrestled with his family's greater one. His words hung like a prophecy of doom that pole vaulting wants to ignore. In another part of the house, dogs barked and young boys roughhoused. It is always that way in February, when the company comes calling, and the Dare house is, at once, both so full and so achingly empty.

5 The M&D Track Club

Inching up "The Hill" to his apartment near the University of Tennessee campus, Mack would point the nose of his 1983 Dodge Omni skyward, grind the gears, and put the pedal to the metal. On good days, a lurch of barely detectible motion would follow, while Mack hunkered down behind the wheel as if to cut wind resistance.

Knoxville, Tennessee, is, among other things, home to the 27,000-student University of Tennessee; site of the last successful World's Fair held in the United States in 1982; the place where director Quentin Tarantino and MTV stuntman Johnny Knoxville were born; the town where Hulk Hogan wrestled when he was known as Sterling Golden; the location of the jail from which Kid Curry, a member of Butch Cassidy's gang, escaped in 1901; and the city where the soft drink Mountain Dew was developed in the 1940s by Hartman Beverages.

During Tim Mack's student days there, Knoxville—with its elevation of 936 feet and the hazy Smoky Mountains flanking it—was as big a problem to Mack's wheezing car as a high bar was to the man behind the wheel. "The Hill," the rising bank on the north shore of the Tennessee River, was the site of the small original campus. Mack's apartment perched atop the neighborhood known as Cedar Bluff. The road to the apartment ran uphill at such a drastic angle it ought to have had a ski lift alongside it.

Coach Jim Bemiller sold the car to Mack for $200 after Tim graduated from the University of Tennessee. The car was an indeterminate color located at the confluence of soot and grime where they form crud. "It had 130,000 miles on it. It was originally white, but it was so dirty you couldn't clean it if you tried. We're talking layers of dirt baked into it. That thing was a death-trap," said Mack.

"His roommates killed him about the car," Bemiller said, "but I knew Tim didn't have any money. That's why I sold it cheap."

"Tim would be sitting so low," observed Russ Johnson, Mack's roommate for five years, "because the seats were about eight inches off the ground."

It stayed low to the ground, apparently, because it was afraid of heights. "Dude, it wouldn't go uphill," Johnson said. "Our other roommate, Andy Knight, had a Dodge Cherokee. Tim's car would only make it up the hill if he had about a 30-mile-per-hour running start. Andy would be in front of us. About halfway up the hill, he would stop, and Tim would have to go back down and try again."

Only once did Mack foil Knight. The Omni was capable of only a move or two on a hill before the engine would meekly agree to surrender terms. "I knew he was going to stop," Mack said, "so I said, 'Screw it.' I veered over the curb. I was half on the grass and half on the street, and I cut in front of him. That was one of the better days. It felt great."

Johnson, Knight, and Mack were all young pole-vaulters in the mid-1990s. In Tim's car, they fervently hoped someday to be old pole-vaulters.

"We would be creeping up 'The Hill' so slowly, it was like we were checking people's houses out, like we were stalkers," said Johnson.

"Tim, we've got to go faster than this," Johnson would plead.

"I've got it floored," Mack would reply.

For Mack, being a graduate student was even tougher than being a little-known pole-vaulter on a one-quarter scholarship. He is the only one of the Macks' five children to graduate from a four-year college. "His scholarship included books but not tuition, and it was high because it was out of state," his mother said.

In 1997, the time of the "Daily Gradual Ascent of The Hill," Mack was working at a packing company. He loaded tea bags, taking little boxes of them off a conveyor belt, putting them in a bigger box, and strapping it tight with tape.

"I hated the smell of that place," he said. "I stood in one place, and I'd work from 4 in the afternoon till 3 in the morning. I was in grad school and still trying to vault. I wondered that it had come to this. I wondered if I was capable of supporting myself to where I could only pole-vault. That was my big dream. I thought about it all the time. Was pole-vaulting all a pipedream?"

Many pole-vaulters give up the sport after their college days. There is no support system around them. Coaching is no longer part of the program, because they no longer represent the university. "When you think about it," said Joe Whitney, the University of Tennessee's sports psychologist, "Tim had no logical reason to still be in the game. He was twenty-three or twenty-four years old, getting up at 5 in the morning to work out, making ends meet with jobs other people didn't want to do."

"One reason I never had a girlfriend [until Grace Upshaw] is I didn't have the means," Mack said. "I was barely able to take care of myself. There was no one serious in my life before Grace. After I started to jump well enough to get the means, I became more open to things."

There was no spare time for a social life. What Mack calls the best day in the Dodge Omni was also the last day in the rattletrap. "I was going to work to pack more teabags," Mack said. "It was icy, and some-one cut in front of me going down the hill. I was going real slow, but I clipped the front end of his car. Then, when I tried to steer back, I turned into a telephone pole. I was going slow enough that I had time to brace myself, so I wasn't hurt."

Mack got out of the car and circled it, surveying the damage. Then he jubilantly pumped his fist. "I totaled that bastard! I'm saved!" he cried. "I don't have to go to work, and I'll never have to drive that damn car again!"

Long before Bemiller sold Mack the barely rolling Omni, he took a special interest in him. They would come to have a deeper relationship than the normal coach/athlete association.

"I was lucky. I had good friends looking after me," Mack said.

It wasn't all luck. Some of it, his friends would say, was his just dessert.

Russ Johnson jumped 18–6 as a Vol, second all-time to the magnificently talented Lawrence Johnson. Russ Johnson only came to the University of Tennessee because he saw Mack at the U.S. Nationals the night after he had jumped at a high school meet at Atlanta's Georgia Dome.

"I went because I had never seen anybody jump 16 feet," Russ Johnson said. "I was 5–10, 140 pounds, and I was told I had to be 6–2, 185 to get a scholarship. Actually, I wound up with an academic scholarship to Tennessee. There were two college guys in the Nationals, and Tim was one of them. He was really skinny then, 165 pounds, tops. He looked like a skeleton compared to now. I think he no-heighted that night. I remember he was throwing his poles around and wasn't happy."

Russ Johnson's father said: "If that guy can make it to college vaulting, there's no excuse if you don't too."

On his visit to the Knoxville campus, Russ sat at the top of the bleachers in awe of the three 18-foot jumpers, who kept going off into the wild blue yonder. "The first person I saw that day was Tim Mack," Russ said. "I was a freshman, and Tim was a graduate assistant coach. He was the only one who walked up to the top of the steps and talked to me. He was interested in me, even though he didn't know me. We talked a lot about my goals. 'You need to come here,' he told me."

Both Russ Johnson and Mack clicked with "B," Bemiller's nickname. "'B' instills confidence and doesn't get rattled," Russ Johnson said. "He's a cool customer who keeps it simple. He doesn't want you to focus on every part of the jump, just the big motor mechanics."

Mack also struck up a lasting friendship with Tim O'Hare. "The reason I'm still living in Tennessee and became anything in pole vaulting was Tim Mack," O'Hare said. "My freshman year, the track coach, Bill Webb, told me things weren't working out. I was a walk-on, and he said I wasn't going to make the team. I thought I was out of there. I wanted to jump, so I was going to have to go to a different school. My chances to improve were limited, because I couldn't jump with the team."

"Stick around," Mack said. "I'll help you."

For close to an hour either before Mack's practice or after, he would coach O'Hare. "The whole year I jumped by myself with Tim coaching me. The next year, I made the team, and I jumped four years at Tennessee," O'Hare said.

Years later, Mack would be Tim O'Hare's best man. In 2004 O'Hare would pay his own way to Athens to signal wind direction to Mack at the Olympics.

After Mack had won in Athens, he didn't change. He didn't think service to others was beneath him. When he returned to Cleveland to celebrate Christmas after the Olympics, a reporter scheduled an interview with him at Baldwin-Wallace College, where Mack would train when home. Mack said to get there late, because he was going to spend the first hour studying the technique of an Ohio high school female pole-vaulter who had e-mailed him asking for help. The voluntary coaching was canceled by a record snowstorm, but the altruistic impulse behind it was still strong.

"Tim and I bonded," Russ Johnson said. "We were similar size, similar backgrounds, similar personalities. We were more analytical than the daredevil stereotype."

"For a long time," he added, "Tim was just scraping by. The first time I went to his apartment, he had four shirts in his closet. I said: 'Dude, you have got to go to a store and get some shirts.' But Tim didn't care. He had a very spartan lifestyle. For example, he cuts his own hair with clippers. Do you know anybody who cuts his own hair unless it's with one of those buzz things?"

"I still cut my own hair," Mack said. "I made a few bucks over the years cutting guys' hair. It's been twelve years since I paid to have my hair cut."

He lived on all the "helpers"—tuna, hamburger, chicken. Also on spaghetti and Ramen noodles. When Burger King had 99-cent Whopper specials, Mack would be the first in line. "You can get pretty full on $2 then," he said.

Mack also was a steady customer at Gus's Good Times Deli on "The Strip," a line of fast-food restaurants and bars adjacent to campus. Originally owned by a Greek, Gus Captain, Gus's would deliver steamed sandwiches on campus until 4 A.M. Today, an autographed picture of Mack screaming in exultation after clearing the bar on his gold medal jump in Athens hangs on the wall there. It joins those of many other mostly male Vol athletes, among them the NFL's Peyton Manning and Willie Gault, and Major League Baseball's Todd Helton, who counted on Gus to steer them safely through the shoals of the hungry wee hours to the happy harbors of cholesterol and saturated fat.

The friendships Mack made then in the years of struggle would be instrumental to him in 2004, the shining season of triumph. It was an e-mail from Russ Johnson to Mack—from one studious jumper who had viewed hours and hours of vaulting videotape in the apartment to another studious jumper who had sat bleary-eyed in front of the VCR—that inspired the notebook in which Mack wrote the performance formula for the gold medal.

"Frankly, it is a good thing Tim is analytical, that he is not the daredevil type," said Tim O'Hare. "I'm glad he's not a wild guy. If he did unusual things, he'd get hurt. Tim twisted his ankle more than anyone I ever knew, and he was always so dramatic about it. If he was a real daredevil, he wouldn't be around."

We think of Olympians, particularly gold medal winners in a spectacular event like the pole vault, as men of elegance and casual grace under pressure. The stunts of the would-be sky kings only reinforce the image. Just as at Malone College, Mack endured a hazing ritual at the University of Tennessee. This time it was diving off the side of an abandoned quarry into the water far below. Mack tied a towel around his neck and went howling down with the terrycloth billowing behind him like Superman's cape when the Man of Steel was on the hunt for Lex Luthor.

"I didn't like doing it," Mack said, "but it taught me that you can ignore your fears. It taught me to keep my focus on the things I needed to do, on the process, not on the event as a whole."

But who knew Superman was a klutz?

When Mack came to the University of Tennessee, it was as a backup singer to the headline act that was Lawrence Johnson. Pole vault aficionados know that Sergey Bubka flew alone at the top of the sport, but for sheer athletic ability, Lawrence Johnson was a respectable second.

Richmond Flowers, a world-ranked hurdler for three years in the late 1960s, probably put the University of Tennessee on the map as a track and field power. Johnson, the most prominent black pole-vaulter ever, reflected how the program had become a star incubator since Flowers.

"Lawrence wasn't a great black pole-vaulter. He was a great pole-vaulter in general," Mack said. "He did some amazing things. He must have had unbelievable strength in his tendons."

Johnson, known as "LoJo" as a play on Florence Griffith Joyner's "FloJo" nickname, began as a high school hurdler. LoJo converted to pole-vaulting because the state of Virginia's best hurdler already went to the same high school in Great Ridge. With the Vols, he might have been the best track and field athlete since Flowers. "If anybody saw us standing next to each other years ago, and somebody said, 'Four years from now, ten years from now, one of these guys is going to be the Olympic gold medalist, ten out of ten people would pick Lawrence," Mack said.

Intimidating on sheer athletic ability, Johnson also brought an arrogance to the sport that made the pole he would prop on his shoulder seem indistinguishable from a chip. "He was always very confident," said Mack. "We started out a little rough in our relationship, because he could be a little loud. But he was just supremely confident. I wish I could be that confident in myself."

It was, Mack thought, a difference in the way they approached life. Mack was a master of containment. Pole-vaulting was a hard, all-consuming endeavor with him. He could spare nothing for frills. Johnson was an R&B artist who wrote songs for the Knoxville band Soja. He sang backup with other celebrity jocks for Bryan Adams at concerts. He was prodigiously talented, brimming over with possibilities. He sometimes competed while wearing sunglasses.

"Lawrence was always very open, and I'm closed," Mack said. "He would always get the crowd involved in it. He would get really animated after a make, although not to Toby Stevenson's extreme. He did things that just freaked everybody out, then he'd look at me and say, 'Don't take it personally.' Being around Lawrence prepared me for how it was going to be out there."

Johnson won the 1993 SEC decathlon. As a senior, he scored points for the Vols in the SEC hurdles. He won the U.S. Olympic Trials twice in the pole vault and won the NCAA Outdoor Track and Field Championships. He was second in the 1997 World Indoor Championships. He won the same event in 2001. He was the silver medalist at the 2000 Olympics. He belonged in the sky the way rockets did on patriotic national holidays. He talked of clearing 21 feet (6.40) in the pole vault, after which he would—like Michelangelo taking up his chisel again because the Sistine Chapel was, literally, the ceiling of painting possibilities—devote his time to the decathlon.

Mack points to Johnson's practice regime in gymnastics class as an example of LoJo's freakish athletic prowess. "Lawrence would do backflips on a trampoline for thirty minutes. Bounce, bounce, flip. Bounce, bounce, flip. We stopped timing him by the number of repetitions. We just went by time," Mack said.

The norm for everyone else in the class?

"Maybe five reps in a row," Mack said.

"Lawrence was a key recruit for us," Bemiller said. "He was a high school phenom. He jumped 17 feet in high school. He jumped 18-8¼ [5.70] when he was nineteen years old, same as Bubka. When he was a senior in college, he jumped 19-7½ [5.98], which was the American record at the time."

The kind of ability Johnson had made him a factor in any meet he entered. Even when he was injured, there was always the chance he could put it together. And Lawrence Johnson was injured so often he kept orthopedists happy for years. In 1994 he suffered a horrific fall, missing the pit and tearing the muscles and tendons off his left foot when he landed. In 1998, while filming an Adidas commercial, he suffered a severe sprain of his ankle. In 2001 he won a meet at Princeton after bouncing out of the pit and landing on his hip on a practice jump. That season, he won the U.S. Outdoor while breaking his right fibula. In 2002 he suffered another ankle sprain and had rotator cuff surgery.

Injuries are a part of the sport. The pole vault takes a ferocious toll on the human body. By the 2004 season, the pole vault would spit LoJo out. It is a cruel event, cannibalizing its young. The Lost Boys can soar, but a career without injury is their never-never land. "Staying healthy is a big part of success in the event," said Bemiller.

Despite their differences, Bemiller liked the Mack/Johnson pairing, thinking that their opposed personalities created a strong competitive unit. "Throughout his college career, Tim was overshadowed by Lawrence. Lawrence was an NCAA champ and a conference champ in the best track and field conference in the country. For a while, Tim tied the Tennessee record, but he was always in Lawrence's shadow. Lawrence was the Alan Webb of track and field in his day, the next golden boy," Bemiller said, referring to the USA's 1,500-meter hopeful Webb, who broke Jim Ryun's high school records.

"Tim wasn't enjoying it at all," Bemiller continued. "The neat thing about the pole vault, though, is that it's up to you when all is said and done."

When Johnson no-heighted at the NCAA Indoor Outdoor Track and Field Championships in 1995, it was up to Mack. "Here came Timmy Mack," said "B," delightedly, "winning it for the Vols [at 18-4¾, 5.61]. That year, Lawrence was the Outdoor champion, and Tim was the Indoor."

Later honored at a University of Tennessee baseball game, Mack found his celebrity, although modest by the standards of other sports, to be disconcerting. His baseball training at St. Ignatius along with his release point promptly deserted him when he threw out the first pitch.

"I zoned out. I don't even know if I was on the pitching rubber," he said. "I looked in at the catcher and proceeded to throw a ball in the dirt that he had to stop by turning his glove over and under-handing it. Very embarrassing."

In some ways, it was Mack's lack of success in comparison to Johnson that would eventually allow him to defy the predictions of those ten out of ten people.

Even his gold medal was overshadowed by the gold of fellow Vol Justin Gatlin in the 100 meters in Athens. Gatlin tested positive for synthetic testosterone in 2006 and was banned for eight years from international track and field. Today, on a campus that has named streets for football coaches Gen. Robert Neyland, Johnny Majors and Phil Fulmer, for football players Peyton Manning and Tee Martin, for women's basketball coach Pat Summit and for women's basketball player Chamique Holdsclaw, there is no "Tim Mack Way." Perhaps this is because for so long it seemed like the road Tim Mack took would go nowhere.

After graduation, Johnson signed with an agent. He would never better the 19–7½ he had jumped at the age of twenty-two. Although most pole-vaulters are at their best roughly from twenty-two to thirty, it would not be until Mack was thirty-one that he finally jumped higher than LoJo's best.

With professional earnings at stake, Johnson was, at least in Bemiller's view, overscheduled. Feeling he was being pushed aside, Bemiller eventually split up with Johnson. "The track and field coach gets the short end in those arrangements," Bemiller said. "I kind of think the coach is important. Tim saw how it hurt me. I think Tim and I both learned something from what happened with Lawrence."

The lesson for Mack was that he needed direction in his life and that only in a structured environment with a detailed plan would he ever soar toward the sun. "Most pole-vaulters don't mature in their technique until their mid- to late twenties," Bemiller said. "They've had some success in college, then they graduate and lose that structure that enabled them to succeed. That was the case with Brian Kelly."

"Maybe they got a job," continued Bemiller. "Maybe they started to work to their own schedule. Tim was the smartest one, the one who realized the best thing was to stay with the structure. It's not real romantic, sticking with the program. But when you would start to see others fall away, Tim Mack kept getting better."

It was hard staying with it after Mack got his degree—with no money; with no car at first, not even Bemiller's clunker; with only the kind of jobs most people don't want to do, backbreaking jobs that raised calluses and lowered pride.

"Was it demeaning?" Mack said. "Sure it was. I had a college degree, and look what I had to do to try to pole-vault. I felt great resentment at athletes who could play golf and who were on *SportsCenter.* They could just be athletes. I was a working stiff."

In the spring, when Tennessee was a picture postcard, with blizzards of dogwoods and bursts of azaleas that would defeat Monet's palette, Mack, his back stooped, his knees protesting, would edge across Bemiller's one-acre lawn, weeding it, combing it, grooming it into an emerald corner of Paradise. He would root out the dandelions, prying up the round, solar disks that studded the yard like planted sunshine.

"I wanted to make it feel like the vaulters were part of an extended family," Bemiller said. "I have two daughters and a wife. Anytime I needed heavy labor, I'd enlist some of the vaulters to help out. I have a fiberglass pool, so I'd get them to sand and paint it. We were having a cookout one day after Sunday school, and I told the wife the pool needed time to cure. She filled it up with water and bubbled the paint."

"That was not a good moment with the pool," Mack remembered.

He would cut down branches and clear brush. "B" would sometimes slip him some money for services rendered, since Mack's scholarship had run out with his eligibility. By the time Mack was in graduate school getting his master's in sports administration, he found that grunt work for his coach was sometimes repaid in coaching sessions.

"It was almost like I had one of those homeless guy's signs, 'Will work for coaching.' I'd be on my hands and knees pulling weeds," Mack said.

"I'd get out there and help him," said Bemiller. "I thought this was different from practice. Practice was a time to focus, not to catch up on each other socially."

Bemiller taught sports law at the university two days a week then coached the pole-vaulters the other two. It was not unusual for "B" to show up to practice in a three-piece suit, fresh from the world of habeas corpus and amicus curiae. "I really respected that," Mack said. "He had his family, his business, his teaching, his church work, and he still made room for me. He'd ask if I wanted to play golf, which is about the only hobby I have. But the tee time would be 6 A.M. or something, because he had to be done at 9 to get on with everything else in his life."

As the relationship deepened, Mack occasionally babysat the Bemillers' daughters. The girls, Kelsey and Gracie, are separated by ten years, with Kelsey being the older. It went better with Mack than with some of the others. "One Sunday afternoon," said Bemiller, "we had ordered pizza, and one of the vaulters—not Tim—came over and fell asleep. The girls paid the pizza deliveryman and everything. They babysat him!"

He worked at the University of Tennessee Student Recreation Center. He was a janitor. If his roommates needed their cars, he would borrow Andy Knight's bicycle to get there.

"I had to be there by 6 A.M.," Mack said. "I had to clean toilets and urinals. Getting outside to sweep the tennis courts was the highlight of my day. There were many times I asked myself, 'What am I doing here?' I was experiencing both ends of the spectrum. I was an elite vaulter who traveled all around the country to participate in meets—I wasn't in European meets yet—but I also had my arm down a toilet."

There were other jobs Mack held that fell somewhat south of "desirable" too. He worked at a driving range, behind the wheel of the range cart, collecting the balls. "I was the guy in the little armored car everybody tried to hit," he said.

He worked at a country club in town "filling buckets of balls for rich guys," as Russ Johnson said. Also, during his two years as a graduate assistant to the coaches at the University of Tennessee, he had a stint as a ticket seller for the Knoxville Cherokees minor league hockey team. He would "cold call" businesses, hawking season ticket discounts. As a graduate assistant has no room to be picky, Mack did what needed to be done.

"There was 'Mascot Night,'" Mack said. "They had all these mascots from around town—Smokey, the Tennessee dog; Pucky, which was the Cherokees' mascot, who was a big black hockey puck with a smiley face. But they needed somebody to put on the costume of the B-97.5 bumblebee."

WJXB 97.5 on your FM dial was not about to go unrepresented as long as Tim Mack was around. He pulled on the suit and skittered out on the ice in street shoes. "It was really hot in there. It smelled of sweat, like a hockey locker room," he said.

A little-known drawback to working as a mascot is that the costumes reek. Cans of fabric freshening spray, such as Febreze, are important tools of the trade. "There was no Febreze," Mack said sourly.

But the biggest problem was not being able to see. "I could only look out one side, through a little hole about one inch by one inch. It was like peeking out a screen door," he said. "Somehow, I wound up at one end of the rink while all the other mascots were at the other end."

After Mack shed the bee costume that night—"And I smelled of sweat even then," he said—he was told to run through the crowd, tossing cardboard boxes containing free slices of pizza to the fans.

Deprivation can discourage a man or make him more determined. Sergey Bubka grew up in Ukraine, then a Soviet republic. While state-supported athletes had it much better than others in the Communist society, it still was never satin sheets and whipped cream. The Bubka in Mack knew that such humble labors made him hungrier. The memory of being the Bee stung.

"It definitely gave me an edge on the Europeans. Their elite vaulters are taken right out of high school and given handpicked coaches. I never had that. I went through years of trial and error. There is no substitute for that."

More deprivation was coming at the 1996 Olympic Trials in Atlanta and their aftermath.

LoJo won the 1996 U.S. Olympic Track and Field Trials in Atlanta at 19–0¼ (5.80). Mack, as much the "other" guy from the University of Tennessee as he would ever be, didn't qualify for the final. It was no surprise. His personal best was a half-foot lower than the winning mark.

"I'm pretty realistic," he said. "Eighteen-six was my best, so I knew it was going to be a challenge. The worst thing was that I was tentative. I tried not to hit the bar rather than to make it. I had no plan really."

Unprepared mentally and unready physically, Mack was left with what he brought with him into Atlanta's Olympic Stadium: his character. "I stayed to watch the final," he said. "If I screw up, I stay and

76 · ABOVE AND BEYOND

Tim Mack, age 11.

Tim Mack, University of Tennessee, 1995. Photo courtesy Tennessee Media Guide.

Tim Mack at the Sea Ray Relays, University of Tennessee, 1994. Photo by Kevin Rohr.

Left: Tim Mack on approach at the Gatorade Invitational, Knoxville, Tennessee, May 1999. Photo by Phil Savage.

Right: In this vault at the University of Tennessee in 1998 Tim Mack would clear the bar at 18 feet 4½ inches. Photo by Phil Savage.

Tim Mack at the U.S. Olympic trials, July 11, 2004. Photo courtesy the Mack family.

Tim Mack's swing up with a good "bend." U.S. Olympic trials, July 11, 2004. Photo courtesy the Mack family.

Tim Mack exults as he clears 19 feet 4¼ inches, the winning vault on July 11, 2004, day three of the 2004 U.S. Olympic trials. Photo by Randy Pench/Sacramento Bee/ZUMA Press.

The gold medal vault. Tim Mack clears the bar at 19 feet 6¼ inches to set an Olympic record and win the men's pole vault final on August 27, 2004, at Olympic Stadium in Athens, Greece. Photo by Michael Steele/Getty Images.

Tim Mack celebrates after capturing the gold on August 27, 2004, in Athens. Photo by Michael Steele/Getty Images.

(L to R) Silver medalist Toby Stevenson, gold medalist Tim Mack, both of the USA, and bronze winner Giuseppe Gibilisco of Italy stand on the winners' podium following the medal ceremony on August 28, 2004, at Olympic Stadium in Athens, Greece. Photo by Toshifumi Kitamura/AFP/Getty Images.

Tim Mack and U.S. silver medalist Toby Stevenson. Athens, August 2004. Photo courtesy the Mack family.

Tim accepting congratulations from his longtime coach and friend Jim Bemiller. Athens, August 2004. Photo courtesy the Mack family.

Tim with his family after the medal ceremony outside Olympic Stadium, Athens, August 28, 2004. (L to R) Sister Chris, mother Arlene, brother Terry, father Don, sister Kathy Haagensen, and brother Dan. Arlene holds the ceremonial bouquet and Don holds the olive leaf wreath. Photo by Tim's sister-in-law Angie Mack.

Tim flanked by his parents, Don and Arlene Mack, on Tim Mack Day at St. Ignatius High School, Cleveland, Ohio, September 30, 2004. Photo © Roger Mastroianni.

suffer. A lot of people wouldn't. I wanted it to sit in my stomach. I wanted it to burn. I wanted to remember what it felt like."

"He was overmatched," Bemiller said. "Different people take different approaches. It didn't surprise me at all that Tim let it burn in him. I knew he would do anything he could every day to get a little better."

With only the graduate assistantship on which to rely, without even a whiff of Olympic glory, Mack began the hardest years of his life. For four years, he worked as a fitness trainer at a club called National Fitness Center, operated by Gus Captain, the man who ran the sandwich shop Mack frequented near campus. Gus would open the fitness club at 5 A.M., and Mack would relieve him an hour later. Gus and his son, John, were another supportive group Mack found just in time. "They worked around my schedule as much as possible," Mack said. "I would ask for time off three days before I was going to leave for South Africa and things like that. I wasn't anything then, but they believed in me."

The job kept him in shape, but his wallet stayed lean and mean too.

"I never got to the point where I thought I was going to hang it up," he said. "But I did wonder if I was going to have the means to the end. From graduation until I won the Goodwill Games in 2001, it was a question of barely making it."

He had no sponsors, so he sent out polite letters into which crept a pleading tone. Contributors could sponsor Mack at any of three levels: gold, silver or bronze.

"Gold level was for a $5,000–7,000 donation per year," he said. "If you gave that much, you got to use my name for promotional purposes. You got a link to my Web site. You got my quarterly newsletter. And I guaranteed a personal appearance.

"Silver," he added, "was for $2,000–5,000 per year. You got everything but the personal appearance.

"Bronze," he concluded, "was for $500–2,000. You got the Web site and the quarterly newsletter."

The letters went to Knoxville's Sea Ray Boats, to Pilot Oil, to the energy snack Balance Bar, to Goody's Clothing in Knoxville, to Mack Trucks, and to Bernie Kosar, the ugly-duckling quarterback who set Cleveland's heart on fire with his play in the 1980s. Mack hoped one Cleveland underdog, the ungainly, cerebral Kosar, would help another.

The results?

"No takers," Mack said. "Not a one. The Mack Trucks thing was a big disappointment. I had high hopes for it. I considered it a natural."

The failures to reply left him to his personal support system: the M&D Track Club. "It's what Tim would put on meet applications," Arlene said. "Tim was the only member. It meant Mom & Dad Track Club."

The Macks spent as much as $8,000 a year keeping Tim's unlikely Olympic dream alive. Then came 1997, when Mack lost an entire season to injury. By its end, he would have jumped forever for the Mom & Dad Track Club just so long as he could jump at all.

The great thing about sports is that they symbolize the ability to overcome hardship. This is where the "life lessons" that are part of every coach's message are learned. Nothing is harder than doing without the sport you love. Tim Mack did love pole vaulting, despite the hard edge his menial jobs away from the track gave him, despite the long years of disappointment and defeat, despite devoting the whole of himself, all his life's work, to clearing a bar, despite the repressive way in which it made him leash his emotions, despite a life stripped bare of adornments. He loved it and, Lord, in 1997, he missed it.

Although he didn't know it at first, Mack had incurred a serious strain of the left high adductor muscle in his groin. There are five adductors, the pectineus and adductor brevis and longus that connect the pelvis to the thigh bone, in addition to the adductor magnus and gracilis that run from the pelvis to the knee. They act to pull the legs together and can be injured in sprinting, twisting, and hurdling. The pole vault is a sport tailor-made for groin pulls.

Mack didn't know what was wrong at first. He went to orthopedists in Knoxville. He saw specialists at the esteemed Vanderbilt Hospital in Nashville. He searched the Internet on his roommates' computers, printing out information on what might be wrong. "No one said it was this specific thing and to do this specific treatment," said Mack. "All they did was rule stuff out."

While he worried and fussed, Mack put himself through various rehab treatments. He had ultrasound treatments, endured massages, and worked with surgical tubing, pulling one end of it with his leg, much as in plyometric exercises. He rode an exercise bicycle with handles he could pull back and forth for some approximation of cardiovascular work. He jogged gingerly.

Mack had always been a man who did everything that was asked and then some. "I think I overtrained," he said. "I pushed it a little bit with the first twinge, instead of resting. I pushed so hard that I couldn't even run."

He could do little. He was alone. Bemiller was busy coaching the University of Tennessee vaulters. "I was basically by myself. 'B' wasn't the one going on the Internet to try to find out what was wrong and making the doctors' appointments," Mack said. "I thought I would never get it diagnosed and never get it healed. I'd be driving home to Cleveland in tears."

He watched video of himself repeatedly, a bird who could only marvel that once he had flown. "I vowed that once I got back, it was over," he said. "The other guys are not going to know what happened."

Quitting was not an option.

"Others might have wanted to get out," he said. "I was not jumping that well then. I had not made much money at it. I could've hung it up. But I thought it was just another test. If there was any blessing in that year, it was finding out how much I loved the sport and how much I missed it."

After almost eight months of rest and rehabilitation, Mack finally received treatment at the Cleveland Clinic that completed the healing process. There, he received a cortisone shot. Cortisone is a steroid, and steroids, of course, became the blight of track and field in the Bay Area Laboratory Cooperative (BALCO) scandal. One of the drug's effects is that it increases the force of skeletal muscle contraction, a definite advantage in making a forceful plant. The pole vault has been relatively unscathed by the steroid scandal, although South African Commonwealth Games champion Okkert Brits tested positive for the stimulant ephedrine in January 2003. Janine Whitlock, the British record-holder, served a two-year suspension ending in 2005 after a positive test for Dianabol, a throwback steroid that was in vogue in the 1970s. Another British pole-vaulter, Mike Edwards, tested positive for stanozolol, the steroid that brought down both sprinter Ben Johnson and baseball star Rafael Palmeiro.

The steroid injection Mack took was legal as a medical treatment. It was also his last recourse. "I was told to rest it another couple of weeks, and it should be fine. I don't think I would have come back so fast without doing the other therapy. Even just walking to the car, it felt better," Mack said.

Mack had learned how much he loved the sport, but he hadn't learned enough about it to reach his ultimate goals. In 2000, an Olympic year, the problems he encountered, the deficiencies he discovered in himself, would reshape him physically and mentally. By the next Olympics, he would become, as rival Derek Miles said in surprise, "a whole new jumper."

Mack is a blend of dreamer and realist. He would grab the greatest prize in his sport in Athens by taking precise notes on what led to failure or what caused success. But pole vaulting is also about the athletic state of grace known as being in "The Zone." Mack could only verbalize it in terms of his beloved golf: "It's like a perfect drive in the middle of the fairway, really hitting it sweet, and when the ball goes off the clubhead, it's really smoking. It's all those things, only nearly 20 feet in the air."

It is about more than numbers; it is about "altius," the "higher" in the Olympic motto. It has an epic quality of grandeur to it. You need movies, you need Dolby sound and whiz-bang special effects to do justice to those feelings, and so Tim Mack became a movie buff.

He liked *Dumb and Dumber,* the 1994 Jim Carrey classic. When Carrey buys a Tennessee orange tuxedo, complete with top hat, he breaks into an impromptu jig. "The Tennessee Shuffle," Mack called it, after copying it and, for a time, breaking into it after big clearances and PRs.

"Tim needs to go back to the Tennessee Shuffle," said Greg Hull. "Showmanship is never bad for a sport."

He liked *Varsity Blues,* with its exhortation to "Play like gods out there!" He liked *Remember the Titans,* with the locker room vow: "Nothing will ever break us apart." He liked *Rocky*—"the ultimate underdog movie," as he called it. He would, in the future, come to love *A Knight's Tale.* But in the year 2000, what he liked most was *Gladiator,* Russell Crowe's Oscar-winning turn as a Roman general/gladiator.

"I was a gladiator for Halloween in 2000," said Mack. "I made the mask, had a sword, bought a little shield."

He and Russ Johnson used the movie as motivation. "Russ made a motivational tape for me where Russell Crowe removes his mask and reveals himself as a great general. We both would watch it when we were roommates to psych up before a big meet," said Mack.

Mack jumped 19 feet (19–0¾, 5.80) for the first time at Chapel Hill,

North Carolina, in June 2000. He was almost twenty-seven years old, a gladiator with the blood and dust of countless arenas on him. For the first time, he had ventured where the sky captains went, to duel them on their blue battlegrounds.

"Tim and I drove a rented Ford Focus down to Chapel Hill," said Russ Johnson. "It was one month before the Olympic Trials. He was so pumped because his mother had told him she would buy him a computer if he jumped 19 feet."

O'Hare said he saw a new level of confidence in Mack after that. But the Olympic Trials that year shook Mack. He didn't feel right going to Sacramento. In retrospect, he would believe he had gotten stale—that he had overtrained and his body couldn't respond.

"I had worked too hard to try to get my speed up," Mack said. "I could feel I wasn't real sharp going into the Trials. I could feel it coming on. I couldn't get on stiffer poles because I didn't have the speed to bend them."

The pole-vaulters always talk about the wind that week in Sacramento and how it took the strongest of jumpers to tame it. Bemiller thought that was the biggest problem. "Lawrence Johnson and Nick Hysong handled the bad conditions in Sacramento," the coach said. "Strength was Lawrence's biggest asset. They were two strong guys and they had a big advantage."

The big shock was that Jeff Hartwig, the American record holder at 19–9¼ (6.03), no-heighted in the preliminaries. Johnson jumped 19–1½ (5.83) to win. Hysong was next at 18–9½ (5.73). Mack was eighth, going out at 18–1¾ (5.53).

"Tim got on too small a pole," Bemiller said. "He didn't get on a big enough pole fast enough, and he never really got into the meet. He didn't adjust to the conditions."

Mack hit the bar going up on his last jump. "It was a fairly decent jump, but so much else was going on that I couldn't adjust," he said.

Both coach and jumper knew serious changes had to be made for Mack to be a real contender. "He needed to improve his strength and posture," said Bemiller. "On a good day, with good conditions, without a tough set-up, he was in the ballpark with everyone else. If the wind was swirling and conditions were tough, he lost his posture. He would lean forward near the end of the run. And he wasn't as strong as the other guys."

"I worked so hard. As the year progresses, I usually move back a step on the runway because I'm stronger, and I'll cover more ground," said Mack. "In 2000 I was moving up on it. Yet I ignored it. I thought hard work would cure anything. After that, I decided I would listen to my body. I decided, if anything, I would be undertrained for 2004."

"That burned in him too," Bemiller said. "You're not getting anything from the pole vault except what you accomplish. You have to come to terms with the fact that it's pretty much for yourself. Sacramento was ten years of his life [at the University of Tennessee] up to that time. He couldn't make that up in money in the next four or five years."

The gladiator needed to be stronger. He also needed to be a better general.

6 Altius

Alone in his torment, Mack boarded the first bus of the day for ANZ Stadium in Brisbane, Australia. It was September 7, 2001, the day of the pole vault final in the Goodwill Games. He had reached the city two weeks earlier, but he was hobbled by shooting pains that coursed up and down the outside of both legs. He had done little since arriving except try to quell the mutiny in his limbs. Cocooned in a headset that was playing electronic music whose repetitious beat nearly put him in a trance, Mack barely noticed the surroundings—the Brisbane River, Moreton Bay, the sky that soon would fill with unfamiliar stars.

Begun in the 1980s by American media mogul Ted Turner as an antidote to the boycott-plagued Olympics, the Goodwill Games bounced between East and West every four years until Time Warner bought them. In Australia, the goal was to capitalize on the sports fervor created by the Sydney Olympics a year earlier. It had already been announced before they began that 2001 would be the last of the Goodwill Games.

In Brisbane, the Games' last hurrah on the international sports stage would be Mack's first. Brisbane began in 1824 as a penal colony, one to which the most recalcitrant prisoners in Sydney were sent. It would be the place where Tim Mack's economic bondage ended.

Pain was nothing new to Mack. It's a constant in pole vaulting. Shoulder pain is caused by the stress of planting the pole and bending it like William Tell ready to core some apples. Leg pain is caused by the effects of the sprint to the box, and the jarring plant of the pole. Pole-vaulters often overwork the legs, particularly, because they are fierce competitors, driven athletes who think they can persevere, push through the curtain of pain, and find the skyway hidden behind it.

Still, Mack was hurt, he was alone, and he was close to broke.

Brisbane also can be a harsh place. One of the biggest land grabs in history took place in the Australian state of Queensland, with the white settlers displacing more than 100,000 Aborigines from over 200 tribes before the 20th century began. Historically, Queensland and its capital, Brisbane, have been havens for conservative, sometimes extremist, politics. Gun owners have inordinate influence.

Its image of a place red in tooth and claw was more than a little dated by the new millennium, but ANZ (for Australia-New Zealand) Stadium still was no place for someone not ready to give his all.

"It was really where I learned to compete," Mack said. "It was one of the last meets of the season, and it tested everything about me: Could I get it together for one competition? Should I have tried to run instead of resting? Could I adequately prepare? Could I still vault without swinging on a pole or vaulting for two weeks? Could I get ready mentally?"

Mack knew he had no stress fracture and that nothing was torn that needed a surgical repair. But he had to manage the pain better. Ten days earlier, he couldn't take two steps without wincing. Bemiller was back in the States. Mack had no one on whom to rely but himself.

"I didn't come all that way not to jump," Mack said. "I had massage and treatments, but I had to be careful. Therapists can overwhelm you and leave no time to calm it down. I used ice and massage. For a week to a week and a half, I'd ice three or four times a day for fifteen minutes each time. I used a frozen ice cup, running it up and down my legs. I took Aleve [an over-the-counter anti-inflammatory] twice a day."

When he walked, it was delicately. He would do nothing rash. He wouldn't jog. He would rest. Two days before the pole vault, he began stretching—still no running, still plenty of ice.

He was literally a stranger in a strange land. He knew few of the elite pole-vaulters well. Many of the men who had been at the World Championships in Edmonton that August were there. Russia's Dmitri

Markov, coming off a jump of 19–10¼ (6.05) in Alberta, the equal of the best anyone not named Sergey Bubka had ever done, was in the field. So was Aleksander Averbukh, an Israeli who had grown up in Siberia and was the reigning European indoor champion. Sydney gold medalist Nick Hysong and American record-holder Jeff Hartwig were also jumping. They had no reason to worry about Mack. Although he led qualifying at the Worlds earlier that summer, it meant nothing. It was only based on fewest misses. Mack had faded in the final and finished ninth at 18–10¼ (5.75).

For a man working part-time as a fitness trainer and who had a drawer full of sponsorship rejection letters and a bumblebee costume in his past, it was not good news. Only the top eight in track and field win payoffs.

"I was hitting my takeoff mark at 13 feet in Edmonton, and there were guys hitting it at 15 feet. Fifteen feet to 13 feet is a big difference in efficiency. I was dumbfounded. I didn't have any more in me," said Mack.

But when it seemed least likely, he would find a reserve in Brisbane he didn't know he had. "I knew it was the last meet of the year, and that was one way of getting ahead," he said. "By the end of the year, most guys are burned out and ready to throw it in. It was a challenge to me to see if I could get it together under those circumstances."

When night fell, so did the temperature. To Mack, that meant jumping weather. "It was a cool night like a high school football night back in Ohio," said Mack. "I don't mind vaulting in the daytime, but I love it at night. I always loved jumping under the lights. It seems to make everything brighter, to define everything better. Athens was like that too, the lights shining down. There's a peaceful air to that."

He felt good in his warm-ups, which included skipping down the track. All athletes in the jumps skip as part of warm-ups. They seek horizontal length in the long jump and triple jump, height in the pole vault and high jump. "I was skipping harder and faster than normal, because I needed to shock my system. My nervous system hadn't been firing for two weeks," he said.

The goal was modest. He wanted to clear one or two bars, since everybody who clears a bar gets paid. He started at 17–8½ (5.40), with $2,000 the reward.

"I felt so much pressure at the beginning of the competition just to clear one bar. I went flying forward on the runway, and it wasn't hurting at all," Mack said in wonder. "I took a running jump off the ground, which is one of the things I had been working on all year."

It had always been his weakness. "I am sure Tim would tell you," Tim O'Hare said, when asked to scout his friend, "that he would like to get a better jump off the ground."

In Brisbane, Mack braced for the howl of pain in his legs, but there was none.

"It was so surprising. I was ready for it to hurt. Instead, I felt really strong, like I hadn't missed a beat. That was when I started feeling it," said Mack.

Halfway through the meet, the jumpers who didn't need it as much, the ones who hadn't grubbed and scrounged for the wherewithal to keep jousting, began to fall by the wayside. In what was the biggest victory of his career prior to 2004, Mack won at 19–0¼ (5.80).

The metric number 5.80 is big in pole vaulting when translated into feet and inches, for it equates to 19 feet. The other "magic numbers" are six meters (19–8¼), 6.10 (20 feet) and, of course, Bubka's record of 6.15 (20–2). To Mack, however, the magic number in Brisbane was 20,000—as in dollars. No longer would he moonlight in odd jobs. Soon, he would have an agent, Chris Layne, with Total Sports in Knoxville, and a Nike contract. The latter was modest by the standards of football or basketball, but only the elite of the elite get even that in the pole vault in the United States.

Mack knew he had to change to improve, and the Goodwill Games victory gave him the means to do that.

"It was huge without a doubt. The feeling was almost the same as it was after winning the Olympics. It was so big for me; I couldn't believe it. It came to $15,000 after they took everything out. For me at that time, that was living expenses for a year," he said.

While American competitors often attributed the Eastern Bloc dominance to state-sponsored use of anabolic steroids, that was only part of the story. The USSR and its satellites devoted more time, money and research to sports training than did the West. With the breakup of the Soviet Union, many great coaches and trainers went elsewhere to make their living. Romanian strength coach Tudor Bompa, a former Olympic rower, became a full professor at York University in Toronto. In

1963 Bompa had devised periodization training. When he immigrated to Canada, he became the Johnny Appleseed of the regimen, spreading the gospel of periodization to strength trainers across North America. Mack became one of his disciples.

"I had made periodization training the biggest part of my workouts in 2001," Mack said. "I wanted to be ready at the end, and I made the Worlds and won the Goodwill Games."

He e-mailed Bompa with the new computer his 19-foot jump in North Carolina the year before had convinced his mother to buy him. Mack also called Bompa on the phone. "I never cared where I had to go for help," Mack said. The theory was new in the United States at the time. Periodization breaks training down into phases called preparation, competition, and transition. Recovery time is built in. It varies the time and intensity of workouts, both to sharpen the interest of the athlete and to target specific areas. Some qualities, such as explosive power and endurance, would be mutually exclusive if simultaneously developed. The theory is that by rousing the central nervous system to a fever pitch, greater gains can be made at specific "peak" times than by repetitive workouts to slab on sheer muscle mass. The ultimate goal was to be at the ceiling of Mack's talent on the night of the Olympic final.

"Bompa convinced me to listen to my body," Mack said. "If I had to slow down on paper, regardless of how my training was going, I did. You build yourself in the first half-cycle, then you reduce the amount of training so your body can super-compensate. You train really hard again, and your body super-compensates for that. You feel better, and you're peaking at the right time."

It is his attention to the recovery aspects of training that has made possible Mack's longevity. Physiologically, he isn't as old as the calendar insists. This is because of his lifestyle and because he doesn't let training erode his body the way it did in 2000. With the view of peaking at the right time, Mack and his sports psychologist, Joe Whitney, devised a series of visualization exercises shortly after the 2000 Olympics. The idea was to use the power of Mack's mind to put him there on the runway, under the stars, by the fire-light of the Olympic flame in Athens. "We worked on imagining what it would be like when I walked into the Olympic Stadium in Athens," Mack said. "I thought he was crazy at first, frankly. I got to where I could close my eyes and see myself brushing by people I knew would be there. I could hear the sounds of the Greek music; I could smell the smells. When I actually did get there, it was no big deal."

In his mind, he had seen himself taking his victory lap in Athens countless times before he actually made the run. "I wanted him to have a sense of not only the competitive environment but also of being in that environment and focusing on the cues he needed to perform," said Whitney, who has been working with University of Tennessee athletes since 1998.

For simple imagery and visualization exercises, Whitney might spend only fifteen or twenty minutes with Mack. For serious talks when adversity strikes, the session might last ninety minutes.

"Most pole-vaulters' cues are kinesthetic," said Whitney. "It's a rhythmic movement that leads into an explosive one. It's also difficult because of the nature of the event. You wait, then perform; then wait and wait and perform again."

At the highest level like the Olympics, the physical abilities of the pole-vaulters are very nearly equal. The difference between them becomes their mental acuity. "Tim has a great ability to play and focus. He is very accurate in assessing his strengths and weaknesses," Whitney said.

Some of the visual imagery was done in what Mack calls "The Ork Room." It is an area in one of Whitney's two side-by-side offices in Stokely Athletics Complex on the Tennessee campus that contains an "Alpha chair."

"It looks like a big, white egg, like Mork from Ork," said Mack.

The chair is acoustically designed and, with its ovoid shape, looks like the makings of a giant's breakfast. The athlete sits inside it, the lights are turned off, and his head is soon wrapped in surround sound. For from twelve to twenty minutes, the athlete listens to either music of his choice or to Whitney's pre-recorded, personalized CDs. It's like having Knute Rockne muttering in your ear about the Gipper.

"Music is an emotional primer," Whitney said. "We practice getting to the emotional state we want the athlete in at the meet."

Mack and Whitney had a past that went back to sessions in a tiny office Whitney occupied at the time. Mack would lie on the floor to do his visualizations because that was the only place where there was room.

"I saw him all the time in '98 and '99," said Mack. "I wasn't getting enough sleep. I was going out late. I was really going nowhere." Whitney and Mack talked about the vision of what Mack wanted to do as a pole-vaulter. It was both specifically outcome-oriented (making the Olympics) and sweeping in conceptual scope. Mack wanted to master the event as much as is humanly possible.

"We took a good look at what was taking him away from that," said Whitney. "We looked at his running, sleeping, eating. He absolutely committed to the lifestyle of an Olympic athlete, and that led to a lot of physical changes."

For Mack, it was almost like undergoing a purification ritual. He stripped his life of adornments until it was almost as bare as the scalp gleaming under the barber's shears he turned on himself. He purged himself of distractions, scoured away creature comforts, and confronted the naked truth that he would never clear a bar fixed against the very sky unless he changed. For additional inspiration, Mack used his new computer to set up an e-mail address that was both promise and challenge, a goad that would urge him on every time he logged onto his Internet server.

"I needed something for Athens," he said. "Obviously, I wanted to get the gold. At that time, I was a Top Twenty vaulter in the world, so I needed something to remind myself of where I wanted to go."

Thus was born the AOL username "Goldnathens."

"I kept it to myself, because I wondered what people would think," Mack said. "When I revealed it, some people didn't figure it out for a while. They thought it meant 'Golden Athens.' I was always taping things to mirrors, inspirational sayings. I'd bet a lot of people never thought I really would be Goldnathens."

There's in Mack something of Midwestern modesty and an "aw, shucks" sensibility. He contains his emotions and doesn't let on that there might be a surprise inside the package. In these years, he mapped out the course he was to follow. It fulfilled his deep need for a controlled environment. "I didn't like going to practice and not knowing what I was going to do," Mack said. "So the practice plans went from a couple of pages to over thirty."

"He set up this program for himself, and he would walk around like a robot," Russ Johnson said. "When he set up Goldnathens, he told me, 'There's no doubt.' He was so pissed about the 2000 Trials, and he was not going to let that happen again."

"I worked on my mental approach too," Mack said. "I was totally engulfed in it. My focus was totally on myself, and I didn't have time for anyone else. I laid out my training program in big twelve-week cycles and posted them in the apartment—twelve weeks for indoor season, twelve weeks for outdoor."

"Three years out, he was so focused on the next Olympics, it was amazing," said Russ Johnson. "We would be talking, and he would look down at his watch and say abruptly: 'I've got to go to bed.' He had a checklist on the wall. Did he drink enough water today? Did he lift? Did he stretch? Did he get his protein? How many guys were doing that three years out?"

Said Whitney: "One of the problems with the lifestyle of an Olympic athlete is that it is not the same lifestyle as your buddies who work in a bank."

Mack would go to bed by 11 P.M. If his roommates were playing computer games or watching DVDs, he would come in and turn the volume down. He was dedicated to it and consumed by it. It represented a totality of commitment no athletes except Olympians experience.

How much is a gold medal worth? Three years without ordinary pleasures and everyday living. Three years with denial and asceticism. Three years that fell short of a biblical prophet's mortification in the desert but not much else. "I cannot tell you how many repetitions I have done when I never even picked up a pole," said Mack. "I would visualize myself going through a jump, and my arms would twitch, and my brain would tell my body to do things, and I'd be moving my arms. I was doing it without physically doing it."

He worked out two or three times a week for two or three hours at a time. He would only make ten to fifteen jumps per week, but he would lift three times each week. He worked with plyometrics, threw the medicine ball, took cold baths, and worked on gymnastics. It was absolute drudgery. Even when he had other jobs, he put himself through the same routine.

In one drill, he would walk into Stokely, the University of Tennessee's old basketball facility and current site of the indoor track facility. He would run, drop the pole, plant it, and visualize himself soaring over the bar. He did three sets—thirty times, then twenty times, then ten. Unsatisfactory visualization meant he had to start over.

"I'd be the only one in the place," Mack said. "You look around, and it's just you."

He had to be deathly sick to miss practice. With more money, he began eating better and consequently wasn't sick as often. He worked hard to build up his "core"—the torso muscles from the shoulders to the waist, the "abs" (stomach muscles), the obliques (side abdominals), the "lats" (principally the lattisimus dorsi, the large flat muscle in the back that works during arm movement), the "pecs" (chest muscles), and the "glutes" (buttocks, hips, thighs).

"You need a strong base, a good platform," Bemiller said. "The back takes so much of the shock of pole vaulting; the abs are critical to keep the legs up."

Doubt became his enemy as much as injury had been. "I would wonder if any of this was ever going to help," he said. "I knew what the European jumpers were doing. A lot of them have their coaches with them all the time. I knew I had to compete with them. I had to do everything they did and more. Everything I was doing definitely did not assure me of anything. But I definitely knew if I didn't do it, I was never going to get there."

He would go to the outdoor track at 10 A.M. "It was the same thing as at Stokely. You're the only one there," Mack said. "No one else is out."

Russ Buller, LoJo and Jim Davis, who would all compete in the 2004 Trials, were training together in Knoxville. Mack trained alone. "I don't think I resented it, but it was a distraction," he said. "I trusted what I was doing rather than try to go with those guys. I thought that if I went, I'd have somebody do my training for me."

Bemiller knew about the training, but he couldn't be there often.

"The gratification all had to be internal," Mack said. "You didn't get the feedback from anyone else of running a better time or making a better jump. You think to yourself: 'That one felt good.' But you were only accountable to yourself. Since I couldn't see it from the outside, I had to feel it inside. That helped me make adjustments. If 'B' was in the stands, that was just an extra."

Mack coached high school boys and girls until the Olympic year of 2004. The coaching, however, was customized somewhat to the needs of one Timothy Steven Mack. He has coached three boys and a girl who went on to win state championships in Tennessee. In the old days, he charged $20 per hour, and the price would drop to $15 each if he had three vaulters.

"I used them as unwitting little guinea pigs," Mack admitted. "If there was something I was working on, I'd have them do it too. Little did they know, but they were helping me too."

At the end of 2001, he was ranked fifth in the USA by *Track and Field News*. After winning the 2002 U.S. Indoor at 18–9¼ (5.72) in the Armory in the Bronx, the meet where he met Grace Upshaw, he finished second in the USA Outdoors. He was ranked second in the USA and fifth in the world.

He became a mimic, watching tape of Bubka and 1992 Olympic gold medalist Maksim Tarasov, who had also jumped 19–10¼ (6.05). "It was just little pieces over time," Mack said. "I had watched the tape over and over again from the Worlds in Edmonton. If you look at my vault from then to now, it's completely different. I knew what was wrong, and I knew people who did it better, so I looked to them to fix it."

The next year was critical. The USOC distributes money to athletes who meet Olympic "A" (automatic approval) and "B" (conditional approval) qualifying standards. But in 2003 Mack would gamble with his newfound and hard-won financial solvency, risking the additional Nike stipend he got as a Top Ten jumper in the world rankings. There were technical changes that simply had to be implemented and mastered.

"I knew I was going to take a step back, because I had to change some things," said Mack. "I was working on pole drops, on leg strength and technique, on foot placement. When my foot hit, I was getting too much back kick."

The term "back kick" describes the pole-vaulter's carrying his leg through and almost giving himself a literal kick in the buttocks. It can be caused by poor running mechanics, such as lack of knee lift, too short a stride, or by carrying too heavy a pole. The cure for it is maintaining an upright posture when approaching top speeds.

Mack would go winless in 2003, with a best jump of 18–10¾ (5.76). It was like Tiger Woods changing the swing that had won the 1997 Masters by a record twelve shots, suffering through the transition the next year and then emerging with something smooth enough to pour over hotcakes yet still powerful enough to wallop most golf courses into obsolescence.

"The big thing was to stay in the Top Ten," Mack said. "If I didn't, my Nike stipend would be cut. I was petering around at seven, eight, nine, keeping my head above water in the IAAF rankings. I was sixth at the

Worlds out of thirty-two guys, and every jump felt horrible. I was leaning forward when I ran, but I was still hanging in there. To be struggling with my technique and still be able to hang in was a big thing."

When the final rankings came out, he was tenth in the world and third in the USA.

"That was it!" Mack said. "That was a major step. I had worked on a lot of stuff. I had struggled. I had taken the hit, and I had made it. That was like a green light."

In a way, Mack was part of a venerable American tradition during those years, that of the lone tinkerer, the solitary man on a quest. One of the sayings he had taped up was a quote from Bob Richards: "Ingenuity plus courage plus work equals miracles."

"I try to live by that," Mack said.

In early 2004 he took a bike tire weighted with sand and dangled it from the pole when he ran. That was to build strength. He devised a sled with which he could run then went to a welder's shop in Knoxville and got him to make it. That was for better posture in running.

He had always been a meticulous record keeper. The so-called "Book," which would give him a reputation as a distinguished scholar of what Bubka called the "Professor's Sport," grew out of his practice of keeping strict accounts. It wasn't really groundbreaking. Edwin Moses, a physics major in college, had used a meticulous, scientific study of the technique of the 400-meter hurdles to become the best in the world in the 1970s and '80s. Mack's "Book" was more like a precise survey of the ground he had covered and a careful log of the implements he had used. Some observers thought it was magical, fashioning miracles out of the thin air. But it was based on empirical results and not mystical vibes. There was no abraca-dabra to it. It was simply assembling and organizing the variables, such as the pole's length, its weight and flexibility, the height of the grip on it, the standards setting, the placement of the marks and the conditions.

"I kept track of Tim and his progress. In the first quarter of the 2004 season, I went to a party with my wife, and when I came back, my mind was racing," said Russ Johnson. "I e-mailed Tim that night."

Russ asked his old roommate and avid golfer if he ever wondered why he could hit eighty balls straight down the middle at the driving range in two hours' practice, boomers going nearly 300 yards, and then the next day, he couldn't.

Mack's PR (19–2¼, or 5.85) was in 2002 at Bubka's meet in Donetsk in the Ukraine. "Can you tell me what you ate for breakfast that day?" asked Russ Johnson. "What was your philosophy for that meet? Were you aggressive or passive? Were you aware of what was going on around you or not?"

"Most pole-vaulters," Johnson said, "might remember only one or two things, like where the standards were on a big jump or what pole they were on then. If they remember one or two variables, that's good."

With tendency tracking, Mack and Johnson set out to do better.

"In a long workout, if I kept track, I'd probably jump better," Johnson said. "There might be ten variables that are not important. The longer you track tendencies, the more you can narrow them down. You can tell yourself you don't need to focus on this one. The pole vault is hard enough to understand anyway. Often, the only person who can understand what you're talking about is another pole-vaulter."

The idea was for Mack simply to trust the numbers that had proven successful over the course of his long years of experimenting.

"Say you come down to your third attempt at 19 feet," Johnson said. "You turn to the chart and see where you stood to start the run for 19 feet, where you needed to grip the pole, the depth of the standards, which pole you needed to be on. When everything was going crazy around you, the idea was you just trusted the numbers and went on autopilot."

In its own way, "The Book" was an expression of the mathematical elegance of the event, just as Georges Seurat's painstaking, luminous pointillism was a breakthrough in art. Systems don't have to be soulless, when they let a man fly. Seurat, like Mack, used analytical precision to systematize his discipline. Opposing hues on the color wheel, such as orange and blue, if juxtaposed, will both be strengthened and intensified when viewed by the human eye. Pole vaulting itself is a balance of polarities—the rugged individualism of solitary tinkering and the support group vital to success; the daring of Icarus and the shields and parachutes to provide a safe landing. For his part, Mack was juggling a number of opposites: brains and brawn, work and rest, past and prelude. The aim was for each element to buttress the other, for the whole to blend into what painting calls masterpieces and pole vaulting calls infinity and beyond as defined by six meters. What began as a sheet of paper became an entire notebook. It attained a reputation as the Rosetta Stone of pole vaulting.

Mack numbered his poles and then trusted the numbers. "Not doing this cost me two SEC championships by making stupid decisions," Russ Johnson said. "I should have stayed on the pole I was on instead of reacting to other people. Lawrence Johnson always told me not to watch anybody else, so you wouldn't be affected by what they do. Tim never watches the other jumpers. He can tell if a jump is good or bad from the way the crowd reacts."

Said Mack: "It was designed for calm conditions. If there's a tailwind or headwind, I make small adjustments. I switch to either a stiffer or a smaller pole. It was appropriate that Russ is from Augusta, Georgia [where the Masters is held]. The golf analogy was very appropriate. I might hit my 8-iron 150 yards with the wind dead, but if it's in my face, I might need a hard 8 or even a light 7. I might think about what I did two years ago, when I made a three on this hole instead of a five last year. I'm not really very good at math, but it gave me information I could trust during a meet."

It was a perfect system for Mack, who could concentrate beyond most limits of human weakness, who was not a "natural," and whose development was the result of hours of practice and minute observation. Then, at the Prefontaine Classic, held only three weeks before the U.S. Olympic Track and Field Trials, it almost all turned to gibberish.

The Prefontaine Classic was named after the late Steve Prefontaine, one of the great figures in American track. Prefontaine at one time held all of the American distance running records. He ran with ferocity. He was seemingly determined to break himself and win no medal at all rather than compromise the totality of his commitment to go gold. He was small, seemingly composed of one part flying hair, one part thick mustache, three parts heart, lungs and astonishing cardiovascular system, and all the other parts pure will. "Somebody may beat me, but they are going to have to bleed to do it," he once said. His method was balls-out on the track, and his lifestyle was the exact same off it. He died at the age of twenty-four in a car crash after a party at which he had been drinking alcohol.

"You always want to do well at the Pre," Mack said. "You can feel his spirit when you step on the track. You know how great he was, how his life was cut short."

Mack finished ninth at the Pre. He cleared only one bar at 18–0½

(5.50). "I didn't understand it," said Mack. "I had gotten last place, but I knew I was on my way. I was getting over the crossbar by so much, it should have come. I was telling my parents all year, 'It's there. I've never felt this good in my life.' But I wasn't clearing the heights."

After the Prefontaine meet, he had received the implement that would help him scrape the sky: a specially designed pole made by UCS Spirit that was stiffer than a morgue. It was hand-delivered to him by Steve Chappell of the Carson City, Nevada–based company. Mack would call it the "Big Stick. The original, which he did not use in Athens, was either stolen or misplaced in the hubbub after he won the gold medal. He used an exact duplicate to jump 6.01 meters (19–8½) later in the season.

Bemiller had flown out for the meet, as had his agent, Chris Layne. It was the first meet "B" had traveled to outdoors. "Flying all the way across the country to get your ass kicked will increase the frustration level," Bemiller dryly noted.

At the airport, tempers flared. Ties fostered over long years between coach and pole-vaulter were fraying. Time was running out on Mack's three-year plan. "It was a heated discussion," said Bemiller. "I was embarrassed that it happened in front of his agent."

Heads spun in the departure lounge as Mack and "B" argued. It was, it turned out, a problem with the arcane language of the pole vault.

"We had gone through the spring," said Bemiller. "He was doing a lot right. He was getting a lot of air on the bars, but he was still coming down on them. He was gripping higher and running faster, but he still was hitting the bars. It was a new place, a new territory, and Mack had never been there before. We had to get it straightened out. This had been going on for three meets. He would either be two feet over the bar and come down on it or he'd be under it."

"Go harder," Bemiller would say.

"I'm doing what you told me!" Mack would flare back.

In person, Bemiller had gotten a feel for the dynamics and momentum that simply couldn't be gleaned from watching videotape. Mack was swinging harder with his shoulders but that wasn't raising his center of gravity fast enough. Bemiller wanted him to get upside-down as quickly as possible, using his hips and his pop-the-whip trail leg.

"If you swing your trail leg to the top, your hips and your other leg will follow," Bemiller said. "He was trying to do it with his shoulders."

The emphasis on the trail leg would also supply momentum up and into the pit. Continuing the momentum is a critical component of jumping high. Doing so moves the center of gravity as fast and as high as possible.

"I think it simplified the vault into a more continuous movement," Bemiller said. "I could see the frustration, so I tried to simplify the vault in his mind. Trying to do too much is detrimental to execution, because there is not that much time to think. The athlete just has to react in the air."

Instead of "swing hard," Bemiller's cue to Mack became "swing fast."

"It sounds simple," said Bemiller, "but it cleaned out the clutter."

The pitch of the argument convinced coach and athlete that both were passionate about getting it straight. The light that teachers look for in their pupils' eyes came on.

"I thought, 'It's over now,'" Mack said. "We were on the same page after all. It was like pouring gas on a fire, like pushing a snowball off the edge and watching it roll downhill. It was the breakthrough."

In the jumps that were to come, the ones that would put him in the history and record books, he would move up very, very fast, working his arms early. Improving his run and plant, bettering his takeoff position, allowing him to use a swing that was faster and more effective—all of this would soon make Mack go up like a man knocking on heaven's door. "Every piece of the puzzle, for me, is critical," Mack said.

The puzzle had become a mosaic.

Bemiller thought Mack had reached the point where he had developed a good balance of all factors—height, runway speed, and swing speed. He was now a very efficient jumper.

"My old football coach said you can't expect the ponies to beat the thoroughbreds all the time, but once in a while you get a pony that doesn't know any better," said Bemiller. "It was a joy to keep challenging Tim to improve, because he is not the fastest, tallest prodigy around, but he accepts the challenge of figuring out how to get better when others have dismissed his chances. He made himself into a world-class athlete, but he was hardly the perfect storm of factors aligning like Bubka. Tim's journey was very impressive and very important to me."

Next, they put the last piece of the mosaic in place.

"We decided to move the standards to 50–60 centimeters [a range between 1 foot–7¾ inches and 1–11½], so he wouldn't work so hard getting to the bar," Bemiller said. "Usually we want the standards as deep as possible, because it's safer and you can be more aggressive off the ground."

That night, Mack called his parents. In exactly twenty-two days, the U.S. pole vault team that would go to Athens would be chosen in Sacramento at the track and field trials.

"I will win the Olympic Trials," Mack told them.

7 The Birdman

The plane droned over what used to be Mother Russia, as it took the world's best pole-vaulters on the final leg of their annual pilgrimage to Donetsk in eastern Ukraine. They sat in their seats with their teeth chattering and their breath frosting in the chilled air. Because there was no baggage compartment, their poles were stacked as high as the seat backs in the center aisle. American record-holder Jeff Hartwig was perched atop them. He is a free spirit who lives in a house with a basement containing 145 snakes—primarily pythons and boa constrictors—plus a copperhead rattlesnake, two iguanas, five turtles, two alligators, and a monitor lizard. Perhaps Hartwig, the American record-holder both indoors and outdoors, was simply trying to channel the spirit of a cat, the better to land on all fours in the event of an emergency landing on the frozen steppes.

"When I saw the photo of Hartwig on top of those poles in the aisle, I almost fainted dead away," said Tim Mack's mother.

The Union of Soviet Socialist Republics has gone into the dustbin of history. The men who aim themselves for the stars come back every February now to Ukraine. They come to Donetsk: the home of Sergey Bubka. In Donetsk, Bubka's startling physical talent combined with the Soviet Union's state-supported athletic system to create the greatest pole-vaulter ever. He nearly flew forever.

"It is a hard-core mining town," said Mack. "It's like what you think Eastern Bloc cities are like—snow, everything else brown or gray, the river frozen."

"The amazing thing about the Soviet Union," Mack continued, "is how primitive their training was. Bubka would run stadium steps with a fourteen-pound weight on his back. Instead of a modern pit, they would use mattresses. Instead of medicine balls, bags full of pebbles."

"The conditions developed strong character," Bubka said. "If you have everything, a beautiful environment, you are not hungry for success. In some ways, this determines what happens but not as much as the value of the success and the dream to the athlete."

When Bubka was four years old, his mother fished him, as he was turning blue, out of the barrel in which she soaked cabbages. The year before, he tried to run away from home in the Soviet city of Voroshilovgrad (now Lugansk in Ukraine). On another occasion, the timely intrusion of a cherry tree branch snagged the boy's pants as he fell like a blossom that had just budded. If a track coach had recruited his school, Bubka, busy playing hopscotch on the desktops at the back of the room, would have been his pole-vaulter.

Bubka moved to Donetsk in eastern Ukraine when he was fifteen, five years after he began vaulting under the tutelage of Vitaly Petrov. The gray, industrial city of five million, the site of the largest indoor track and field center in Ukraine, is brightened in its smoggy pall by the rose bushes that thrive amid the slag heaps from the coal mines.

Because of Bubka, Donetsk would soon be to pole vaulting what Tennessee State University, home of Wilma Rudolph, Madeline Manning, and the Tennessee State Tiger Belles, was to women's track in the USA in the 1960s. Donetsk was the world headquarters of fiberglass-assisted flight. Because of Bubka's prowess, the joystick came to track and field long before it did to computer games.

The journey to Donetsk for Bubka's Zepter Pole Vault Stars meet is not a business trip for Mack and the others. It's an homage.

"I fly from Atlanta to Frankfurt to Kiev. Then you take a puddle-hopper that Bubka charters to Donetsk," Mack said. "It was freezing cold inside the plane. We got into Donetsk at 10 at night. We had all been traveling twenty-eight to thirty straight hours. All we wanted to do was take a hot shower and go to bed, and there was no hot water. I guess they turn it off after 10."

Yet even their stories about the perils of travel contain a core of deep respect. "The mattress might be thin in the hotel. But it's all right. You're going there to see Sergey," said Toby Stevenson.

"The most interesting thing is his mind-set," said Mack. "After the competition, we would always watch a ballet. Then, we would go upstairs for a banquet and awards."

Bubka said: "After a competition, your mind is stressed because you have been focused so long. Get away! Relax!"

"Whoa!" Mack said. "That is exactly how I felt."

Mack theorized that Bubka loved ballet because it's so much a part of the culture in nearby Russia. Perhaps there is more to it, though. The pole vault is the most spectacular event in track and field, a visual of power and grace that fires the imagination. Mack's coach, Jim Bemiller, calls the pole vault a "violent ballet." Perhaps Bubka is Nureyev in spikes.

At the Donetsk meet, Bubka visits with the invited pole-vaulters at a dinner at his restaurant. He spends only two or three minutes with each vaulter, but it has the same allure to them as talking hitting with Ted Williams had to generations of major league baseball players. It's like golfers getting to talk to Jack Nicklaus and asking: "What's up with my swing?"

"We put him on a pedestal," Mack said, "but you can sit down and talk to him like any other vaulter." The meet itself is pole vaulting crossed with MTV. Spotlights sweep the arena. It is sports as video games, sports as rock concert. But the non-competing host, Bubka, would be the one who was greeted by flaring waves of flashlights and cigarette lighters. The pole-vaulters compete on a wooden floor. Music thunders through the small hockey rink, which seats only 4,800. The choice of tune is up to each vaulter.

"I'd play 'Lose Yourself' from *8 Mile*," Mack said. "The first time I went, I was extremely pissed off. I went out early, and Tim Lobinger [of Germany] wanted to know if he could use my music. I thought it was my song."

Eminem's song spoke to Mack with a pulsing beat that got into his blood. It started as motivation and became the story of his life. It is about seizing the day, a competitor's "one shot" to maximize an opportunity that may not come again.

It was in Donetsk on his first visit that Mack first heard the music from the movie *A Knight's Tale.* "The theme of the meet was that you were being knighted," Mack said. "The music was from the movie. Being a knight really appealed to me. When you carry the pole, it's kind of like jousting, so I saw the movie as soon as I got home."

The second time Mack was in Donetsk in 2002, he set a personal best (PB) at the time of 19–2¼ (5.85). "I felt inspired getting an invitation from Bubka," Mack said. "That was when Hartwig jumped six meters. At the time, it seemed very far away to me. As for my PB, I didn't want to disappoint Bubka, didn't want to disrespect his turf."

Knighthood flowered along with the roses in the harsh land. "You could see how Bubka got so tough. That place would toughen anybody up," Mack said.

Bubka was ten years old when he first picked up a pole. It was like King Arthur drawing the sword from the stone. While many pole-vaulters don't peak until their twenties or even thirties due to the extremely technical nature of the event and its enormous physical demands, Bubka profited from the same, consistent model of technique from his formative years onward.

"I got all the information I could on the event. I read all I could about it. It is a tough, hard event. But it is also very pleasant. I devoted everything to it. It was my life," he said.

At the 2004 Olympic pole vault final, Guiseppe Gibilisco of Italy said, "To pole-vault, you must be a little bit crazy." Gibilisco's words play into the rakish image of pole-vaulters; his words also anger Bubka.

"I don't think that is so," he said. "You must be very clear thinking. You must be a very intelligent man. There are so many qualities: the pole, the grip, the standards, the weather, the plant, the takeoff. You must be a professor."

Bubka would go over the bar in what he calls "The Professor's Sport," screaming like an eagle singing to the wild sky. No wonder the Europeans called him "The Birdman." Once Bubka was identified as a man who could fly, he traveled with the renowned Petrov as his vaulting coach; Aleksandr Solomahin as his gymnastics coach; and Boris Tulchinsky as his sports psychologist. Petrov once said a pole-vaulter had to learn the "culture of movement." No one ever busted moves like Bubka.

Bemiller noted that the Polish coach Andrzej Krzesinski, who developed the 1976 and 1980 Olympic gold medalists, likened the training process to charging a battery—a slow input over a long period of time eventually amounting to juice enough to electrify the sky.

Mack—obsessively filling his notebook, a tinkerer building a better mousetrap, the knight with no cities sacked or booty looted to give him fame—could never match the Eastern support system, except in an unbending determination to overcome the obstacles in his path.

"I had strong coaches all the time," Bubka said. "I do not understand why in the USA pole-vaulters are often by themselves. Psychologically and physically, you need coaches to control what you do, to change this exercise or make that one more important."

No one has flown higher. No one has ever completely dominated the pole vault. But Bubka came close. He won six World Championships, the first at nineteen years of age. In Helsinki, while most of his competitors complained about the conditions, Bubka took the inaugural World Championships in 1983 by storm. Tianna Madison, a long jumper from suburban Cleveland like Mack, was the only other teenager to win a world title in a field event.

Bubka deserves mention with Carl Lewis and javelin thrower Jan Zelezny of the Czech Republic as the greatest field eventers ever. Lewis won four Olympic long jump gold medals but never held a world record in it. Bubka won only one Olympic gold, but he produced world records like the Ukrainian steppes produced wheat. Zelezny was a world-class javelin thrower for twenty years until his retirement in 2006.

In the pole vault, only Cornelius Warmerdam rivals Bubka. Yet mystery cloaks the reasons for Bubka's prowess. History becomes his biggest opponent. Bubka's records have outlasted even those Warmerdam set before World War II. Warmerdam's mark of 15–7¾ (4.77 meters) lasted fourteen years. Undefeated from 1983 to 1990, Bubka set thirty-five world records—eighteen outdoors and seventeen indoors. His outdoor mark of 20–1¾ (6.14 meters) was set in 1994. His indoor mark of 20–2 (6.15) was set in 1993 at Donetsk. Twenty feet (6.10) remains a threshold only he has crossed.

There is a drawback to the event's minimalism. The records climbed by the tiniest increments, centimeter by centimeter. A bonus from the Soviet Union of $385 in rubles accompanied each world record. In the glasnost era, it rose to almost $3,000 for each record. When the free market arrived, Nike bumped that up to $100,000 for each one.

The record advanced by the breadth of a gnat's wings. The argument can be advanced that Bubka was thrilling more crowds and giving more fans lasting memories of the event. Yet it was hardly in keeping with the "altius" spirit of the sport. The ultimate irony is that Icarus soared higher only a pinfeather at a time.

Bubka was the greatest young pole-vaulter, the greatest pole-vaulter in his prime, and he was a good enough pole-vaulter in the twilight of his career to make the Sydney Olympics at the age of thirty-six.

Like other pole-vaulters before him, such as Richards and Lawrence Johnson, Bubka could have been a magnificent decathlete. He ran 100 meters in 10.2 seconds, long jumped nearly 26 feet, and threw the shot 44 feet. He never considered surrendering the pole and living his life earthbound. "I know he beat Yuriy Syedikh, a two-time Olympic gold medalist in the hammer throw, in the shot put," said Steve Chappell.

"He was the strongest mentally," said Mack. "No one else has had the total package. My focus mentally is as great as his was. If I was a little faster and more powerful, I might vault 20–2. I'm not even close to him physically. Speed kills, as in any sport."

Said Kory Tarpenning, once the best pole-vaulter in the United States: "It's the amount of force he was able to generate. He put 10 to 15 percent more energy into the pole, which is why he went higher than anyone else."

"Other guys vaulted with stiff poles comparable to Sergey's," said Chappell. "Others had similar physical abilities, but he was the whole package, mental and physical, plus all that drive and ambition."

Even with better poles, more widely disseminated technical information, bigger and faster jumpers, and increased reliance on video study and computer modeling, Bubka still flies solo. Professor Bubka specialized in audacity. He could bend a pole designed for a man forty pounds heavier. The pole-vaulting maxim, playing off a hit movie about soccer, is: "Forget Beckham—bend it like Bubka."

Former NFL tight end Todd Christensen, doing track and field commentary when Bubka first cleared 20 feet, called him "the world's most under-exposed athlete."

A light payload at 6 feet, 175 pounds on a powerful catapult, Bubka went shrieking over bars at which others could only kick impotently with their feet. Estimates are that he could have cleared 20–6 (6.25) or even higher had the bar been set that high. "How much is mental, how much physical?" asked Bubka. "There must be a balance. You cannot simply condition yourself to be physically better than anyone else. You have to be physically fit, stable psychologically, and you still have to have the technical skills. My personal characteristic was to improve myself in everything, in will, in technique. You must be very focused on it all twenty-four hours. You must be very careful away from the runway."

His life was a battleground. The professor fought with the daredevil. The aloof, tranquil Bubka, sitting alone, would arise and attack the vaulting box like a soldier taking a pillbox. He laid siege to the sky. The victory cry as he streaked over the bar seemed to explode like a firecracker because such stillness preceded it. Perhaps going to the summit in anything makes a man shout at the glory of it.

In Bubka clashed brain and brawn, art and sport, mercenary and Communist, privacy and publicity. The synthesis he developed from the opposites linked earth and sky. He is a great sportsman, and yet some pole-vault coaches suspect Bubka was the driving force behind the IAAF's decision to outlaw Volzing. Bubka cleared bars like Michael Jordan cleared rims; of course, pole-vaulters think, he would have wanted stubbier pegs for the crossbar.

Ed Dare feels only Bubka could be trusted to study the soft boxes thoroughly, lest they turn out to provide a boost to those who seek his records.

Lawrence Johnson once told of a meet in Sestriere, Italy. LoJo asked for and received a pointer about his takeoff from Bubka. After correcting the takeoff problem, Johnson asked Bubka another technical question. "All of a sudden, he didn't admit to understanding English," Johnson said.

In a speech Bubka gave in Budapest in 1997, he addressed part of his contradictions. "I had to learn to be reserved," he said. "To waste no energy that could be used in competition. By the time I was 15, I had left my family and was staying with my brother Vassily at the sport school in Donetsk. Once, I went to the grocer to buy 100 grams of cheese [about 3½ ounces], but the woman behind the counter tried to give me just ninety grams. She wanted to cheat me. Now I lost my temper. I felt outraged, because I had been brought up to be honest with people.

"But later," he continued, "I was told: 'Don't explode. Don't waste your nervous energy on these things. You must learn to focus that energy into competition. Give it a good channel.' As I got older, I began to avoid anything that was too much of a distraction. I realized that I was sensitive by nature and that sometimes I let things affect me. For example, I try not to spend too much time with journalists or even making speeches."

Few men have been such icons with so many followers eager to sing their praise.

"Bubka is 'The Master,'" said Toby Stevenson, the silver medalist in Athens. "He was the Nolan Ryan, the Michael Jordan, and the Walter Payton of pole vaulting."

"Bubka is 'The Man,'" said Mack, the gold medalist.

Few men have had such iconoclastic peers eager to debunk their image either. "It's hard to be complimentary of Bubka," said Bob Richards. "I'm talking about steroids and all the stuff the Russians used. The East Germans were all on steroids. The Russians in Bubka's time were too."

"You tell me," said Don Bragg, Olympic gold medalist in 1960. "What was Bubka on? I'm not saying he still wasn't great. I'm a guy who wants to legalize everything. You get tested by doctors, and if you have any liver or kidney problems, you get shut down for a while. At least everybody would be honest then."

Except for the women's javelin and the women's pole vault, men's and women's field event world records are a decade old or more. There is no doubt that more rigorous drug testing today is the primary reason why.

The contrasting views on Bubka's marks seem to result from a generational split more than anything. Richards and Bragg—the Cold Warriors, men whose worldview was formed and whose athletic glories were secured in the first years after World War II—knew Eastern Bloc athletes as personally engaging, but they thought the system that shaped them was corrupt.

Mack and Stevenson—younger men who were in high school or middle school when the Berlin Wall fell—grew up with the old Soviet Union reduced to a fragmented squabble of small states, with shadowy Arab terrorists as the national enemy, and with Bubka's picture on their bedroom walls.

"Bubka faced those questions because he grew up in the Soviet system," Mack said. "With his speed and jumping ability, there wouldn't be any doubts about why he jumped 20–2 if he weren't from that system."

"Anytime you do anything outstanding, people will assume you're on drugs," said Stevenson. "They said I was on drugs when I jumped six meters. They said Tim was on drugs when he jumped so well late in the season. Tim and I proved you don't have to be on performance-enhancing drugs to jump high. To me, Bubka proved that you don't have to be on drugs too. To me, he was clean. He had the skills, the talent, the instincts."

Bob Seagren, who served as a transition between the eras, takes the middle ground. "Who knows? Bubka was inconsistent in the big meets," said Seagren, the Olympic gold medalist in 1968. "He either set a world record or no-heighted."

"In my era," Seagren added, "there was no testing. Dianabol was the big steroid then, but everyone thought it was just the big weight lifters and throwers. The one I was really suspicious of was FloJo [Florence Griffith Joyner]. Your body does not change that much at that age. No, I am sorry, it doesn't."

Griffith Joyner died in 1996, at 38. As a child, she had ground up crayons, mixed the bright dust with nail polish, and painted her nails like rainbows. She went from a silver medalist as a curve runner in the 200 in the boycotted Olympics of 1984 to the best female sprinter in history four years later at the age of thirty. Many believed to her death that she was one of the first users of HGH (human growth hormone). She could never outrun the dark shadows behind the rainbow.

"It comes down to the doctor," said Mike Tully, the silver medalist in the pole vault at the boycotted Los Angeles Olympics of 1984.

"People can judge my place in sports history for themselves," said Bubka. "I set thirty-five world records and won six World Championships and an Olympic gold medal. I won everything, and my career lasted so many years. I have a great legacy."

He was always tested for doping, as were other winners. He always passed. He passed tests and set records years after Florence Griffith Joyner had retired and sprinter Ben Johnson had been disgraced. "You will always have suspicions that this guy is using. You wonder what that guy has figured out," Bubka said. "We had a system that produced champions in the Olympic Games. We had a system of tests, too. I don't know how many drug tests I took, but I passed them all. The only ones I judge are the ones who have been caught. Suspicion will always exist."

It's the curse of drugs in track and field that belief and doubt go hand in hand. Awe belongs today only to the innocent. Bubka's greatest jump in the clutch, the one that won his only Olympic medal, at once convinced many of his greatness and emboldened his doubters.

Sergey Bubka seeded the clouds. He was so good, he also sowed suspicion.

Told that today's American pole-vaulters consider him "the Babe Ruth of pole vaulting," Bubka said: "Can you explain who this person was?"

It is, in many ways, an apt analogy. Baseball is a sport characterized by failure. Even the best batters fail two out of every three times. In the sport's best-loved poem, the mighty Casey strikes out. The pole vault is a sport that can no more be mastered than a slider low and away on the corner can be hit consistently. It says something about the contrarian nature of pole vaulting that it's designed to break the hearts of those who love it most. You almost always fail on your last jump, even if you've won a meet, even if you've won the Olympic gold medal, because the quest is always to go higher.

"It's a very cruel sport," said Greg Hull. "You can do fifteen things right, and the one thing you do wrong knocks the crossbar off."

Bubka chased the Olympic dream his entire competitive life. He won only the one medal. "It's the nature of the event," said Mack. "So many things can go wrong. He did get an Olympic gold medal the first time he got a chance at one."

Olympic years were never normal. When you devote your life to a sport, you take the rough with the smooth. The injuries, the no-heights, the effects of age in clipping his wings—Bubka can accept that. Political meddling he cannot. "I was more disappointed in the Los Angeles Olympics than anything," Bubka said. "The boycott was so painful."

The USSR and its political satellites boycotted the 1984 Olympics in retaliation for the USA pulling out of the 1980 Moscow Olympics in protest of the Soviet invasion of Afghanistan. "There was nothing we could do about this stupid decision," Bubka said. "We suffered, the athletes. I think it was my time. I was in good shape. It would have been easier then than later. [Winning a medal] would not have become something I did not do."

He set world records shortly before and soon after the 1984 Olympics. It amounted to a declaration that whatever happened in Los Angeles, it was a consolation prize because he wasn't there to beat the eligible jumpers.

Bubka was an overwhelming favorite in Seoul in 1988. He was in the midst of a seven-year unbeaten streak. Mack doesn't believe in "psych" jobs, but Bubka developed a strategy of almost passive intimidation. By 1988, Bubka wouldn't even begin jumping until the bar had climbed to eagle's nest heights.

In Seoul, Bubka's rival, Rodion Gataullin of the Soviet republic of Uzbekistan, took the lead at 19–2¼ (5.85). Bubka's strategy usually was to pass except for three heights—5.70 (18–8¼), 5.90 (19–4¼), and whatever constituted the meet or world record at the moment. He started high and minimized his attempts. He took only four jumps in setting his last world record. In Seoul, he had only one clearance, at 18–8½—and that on his second try. He passed until 5.90. Shockingly, Bubka missed twice. He faced the biggest jump of his life standing in fourth place.

"The third attempt is more exciting," Bubka said. "The psychological strength has to be more. The Olympics are so much bigger than anything else. The stress was much higher. This becomes the prize, the challenge."

Bubka seized a longer pole than he normally used, one that was harder to control. He flashed down the runway and planted like a knight who had speared the dragon on his lance. He went screaming over the bar, scraping the sky, the jump so big it beggared belief. It won the gold medal while raising both possibilities and questions.

"I was in Seoul when Bubka won," Richards said. "He cleared 19–4 by a foot. It was unreal."

FloJo, Ben Johnson's 9.79 in the 100 meters, Bubka—there was a lot of that unreality stuff going around. Johnson later tested positive for steroids and was stripped of his gold medal. "Johnson was the only one they *caught,*" said Richards.

Bubka's jump in Seoul was all or nothing at all. "I was out of medal position. Timothy Mack's third jump was a little different in Athens. Timothy knew he had a medal," said Bubka. "My motto was always, 'when you have an attempt left, you never lose. You have not lost.'"

He never won again in his three remaining Olympics. "Would I rather have a world record or an Olympic gold medal?" Mack mused. "It's a tough question, but I would go with the gold medal. Someone can always take the record away."

The most unexpected failure by Bubka came in Barcelona in 1992. As in Seoul, he passed until 18–8¼. With time running out on his first vault, he rode the pole beneath the bar. American pole-vaulter Tim Bright, mindful that Bubka was often given more than allowable time by European meet organizers hungry for world records, had asked officials to keep Bubka on the clock like everyone else. "In Barcelona, they certainly didn't give him too much time," said Mack.

On Bubka's second vault, he went into the air, riding the solar wind, but brushed the bar off on the way down. Rattled, Bubka passed to gain time. At 18–10¼ (5.75), he switched to a softer pole because of the wind. As he stood on the runway, the wind suddenly died. On the wrong pole, with the clock ticking, he hit the bar on the way up.

Bubka blamed bad biorhythms for what was his only loss of the year. Russian Maksim Tarasov won at 19–0¼ (5.80).

To his critics, Barcelona, almost as much as the never-confirmed drug rumors, clouds Bubka's reputation. Coddled by meet promoters, playing by rules bent more grotesquely than his pole, Bubka couldn't cope with the Olympic imperative to peak at the right moment and to jump now.

In 1996 in Atlanta, Bubka withdrew because of an inflamed right Achilles tendon when he was a slight favorite. In retrospect, his achievements might have been even greater had his last years not been plagued by leg problems that required surgery. In 2000 in Sydney, he failed to qualify for the final, missing all three tries at 18–8¼.

"There was the boycott," he added. "There was the injury. In Barcelona, I was at fault. I needed to be better. You must accept this sometimes. Sydney, I suffered during the season, but I made it there. I did my best. I respect the Olympics too much to have any regrets."

Sometimes, Bubka credits the gymnastics he learned for allowing him to go up like the high note of an anthem. Other times, he credits the technical mysteries of the plant and takeoff. For whatever reasons, no one flies like he did.

Bubka admits he didn't expect, all these years later, to still be world record-holder. "The guys jumping today should have jumped 6.30 [20–8] by now," he said. 'It comes down to the energy transferred to the pole. This is what Petrov knew. They need to focus on that."

Said Petrov in 1985: "A pole-vaulter is, in fact, born in the last steps of the run up; the ability to perform the concluding part of the run determines the ability of a vaulter to perform vaults."

Russian pole-vaulting is, to borrow Winston's Churchill's description of the Soviet Union, "a riddle wrapped in a mystery inside an enigma." Track and field coaches in the USA buy books that try to demystify the Russian theories.

Pole vault coach Rick Suhr in Churchville, New York (near Rochester), developed 5-foot-6 Mary Saxer, a proficient long jumper who had reached 19 feet, into a 14-foot pole-vaulter and a national girls high school champion after coaching her for only one year. He also developed an All-American in Tiffany Maskulinski, who stood only 5-foot-2. Finally, Suhr coached a U.S. Indoor champion in Jennifer Stuczynski, who cleared 15–4¼ (4.68) in early 2006, the highest by an American woman not named Dragila. Stunningly, she flew that high in only fourteen months with Suhr. Russia's Yelena Isinbayeva, the dominant female vaulter today, and Dragila took seven years to vault that high. Russia's Svetlana Feofanova, the next fastest learner on the pole's curve, took four years.

Stuczynski's background was similar to Mack's. She attended a small, Christian liberal arts college, Roberts Wesleyan in Rochester, New York, which was a part of the NAIA. She played basketball, hurdled, and threw the javelin before Suhr, with his practiced eye for outstanding athletes, recruited her to the technical rigors of pole vaulting.

The conditions are primitive, with the training facility amounting to little more than two big, fabricated metal huts, placed end to end, which Suhr built over a pole vault pit. "The huts open to an area where the pit is, with maybe 10 feet on either side. There are two propane heaters, and one of them actually works," said Stuczynski. "It's as cold in there as outside but without the wind chill."

Suhr has acquired a reputation as a man who understood the "Russian style."

"I've had everything given to me in terms of technique," said Stuczynski. "I just need to perfect the model."

Bemiller is skeptical about the East European aspects. "It shouldn't be that hard to turn a 19-foot long jumper like Mary Saxer into a 14-foot [4.27] pole-vaulter, given the size and athletic ability involved," he said, although this does not account for the rise of Maskulinski. "Suhr's athletes may be conceptually attempting the Russian technique but may not look like it, now or ever."

Lawrence Johnson went to a Russian coach after jumping 19–7½ as a collegiate senior, seeking "The Secret." He never jumped higher than he did in school.

The fact is that no one in the Western world really knows how the Soviets did it, if you discount doping.

Said Bemiller: "From my perspective, the defining characteristics of the classic Petrov/Bubka vault would be very disciplined run mechanics with great detail on the pole drop, an outside takeoff spot, and a fast, 'gymnastic' swing. Coaching from an early age emphasizes running, jumping, and swing mechanics."

The Russian style, Bemiller said, "is to have a continuous chain of motion. It's very gymnastic." American coaches have studied Petrov's paper on Russian techniques ever since it was published in 1985. There are, however, many ways to get over a bar. The French developed four Olympic medalists, two of them winners of the gold, between 1984 and 1996 with their own unique style. The so-called "tuck-and-shoot" style, which also featured widely separated hands on the grip, is no longer in vogue even in France. Jumpers were too slow coming out of the ball into which they had curled themselves, their knees against their chests, while the pole straightened.

But unlike the French or the Russians, the United States really doesn't have a national style. There's no standardized national training, no technical style that develops from pooled information.

"There is no U.S. style," said Bemiller. "We have a lot of athletes who are very competitive, who try to beat the heck out of each other, and who have studied the event very closely. Yet they help their buddies out at meets. It is the damnedest process."

The biggest problem with the Russian style is that no one knows what Bubka was like at a young age. No one in the West knows how long "The Secret" was incubating. Film of Bubka before the 1983 Worlds is unavailable. For her part, Isinbayeva, before morphing into the ultimate example of pole-vaulting technique, was supposed to have been on poles that were too small, teetering on the very edge of control, as late as 2002.

Bemiller thinks good mechanics are good mechanics. He thinks fiberglass experimentation led to a drift in the USA from the fundamentals, much as a dunk-centric culture in basketball made the boring old jump shot a lost skill.

"America is the land of the free and the undisciplined," Bemiller said. "Pole vaulting is not a major concern nationally, so kids get into the event because they love to jump. There is no basic instruction in running and jumping mechanics or gymnastics basics. When Tim Mack improved his run mechanics and pole drop, he was not emulating the Russian method, he was doing what he was working on for ten years at Tennessee and overcoming old habits."

Bemiller sensibly concludes that Petrov must have studied rigid-pole jumpers such as Richards and Warmerdam as well as modern pole-vaulters such as Mike Tully, Earl Bell, and Tom Tellez.

Perhaps all of Bubka's vagueness is intentional. There is always the chance it is another Bubka "psych" job, veiling his prowess, planting doubt in the minds of the men who seek to emulate him. Today, Bubka is an influential figure in both politics and international track and field. He is a member of the Ukraine Parliament, in the same party as that of Viktor Yanukovych, the former leader who tried to steal but eventually lost the national election in 2005. Politics is so savage in Ukraine that President Viktor Yushchenko was poisoned with dioxin during the campaign. Bubka, however, exists in his countrymen's eyes on a level far above grubbing for votes. When he retired, he was made an official "Hero of Ukraine." He funded the Zepter meet mostly out of his own pocket, although Nike also contributes. In June 2005 he was elected president of Ukraine's national Olympic committee. He replaced Yushchenko, who is under investigation for using budget funds to reward Ukraine's Olympic winners in Greece.

Bubka is also a member of the International Olympic Committee. "The Europeans put him on it. I hear he's a big cheese," said Richards, sarcastically.

In the Soviet days, Bubka feuded with the government, once saying: "They did not want to have many examples of thinking athletes. It is better to have stupid sportsmen, young ones who do not know what is going on. Sports life is very short. They [the Soviet regime] discarded older athletes and took new ones, and they used them for the system. My policy was just to give good things for sports in my region."

The breakup of the Soviet Union in the early 1990s was a tectonic shift in the pole vault. It created a diaspora of sky jumpers. Aleksandr Averbukh, for example, immigrated from Siberia to Israel in 1999. Dmitri Markov is today probably the best of the male Soviet pole-vaulters who were born in the mid-1970s.

In the United States, track and field is a quadrennial sport, followed closely only in Olympic years. The American production line of Olympic champions fell silent from 1968 until 2000. Now there is a revival in the pole vault, keyed by the popularity of extreme sports and the presence of Americans on the top two steps of the medal podiums at the Sydney and Athens Olympics.

Bubka envied Mack and Stevenson's rivalry. Carl Lewis needed Mike Powell in the long jump, which he dominated even more than the sprints. In the 1960 Olympic decathlon, Rafer Johnson needed C. K. Yang. Bubka only fleetingly had rivals. "Timothy and Toby have all they need to achieve," he said. "They have one to push the other. I did not have this."

Only rarely was he pushed for world records. France's Thierry Vigneron was the bronze medalist at the boycotted 1984 Olympics and a four-time world record holder. He set a record only once after Bubka's ascent, and then he held it for less than ten minutes. Vigneron jumped 19–4¼ (5.90) to take the outdoor mark in Rome, shortly after the 1984 Olympics, but Bubka came roaring back on his next try at 19–5½ (5.93). It was as close as the pole vault gets to "posterizing" a basketball defender with a dunk. Ever since then, Bubka has held the outdoor world record, inching it ever upward.

Bubka didn't like not holding records. They made him the North Star of the sport—eternal, unwavering, the one fixed point that gave everyone else a sense of place. Which was, of course, well below his.

Brazilian vaulter Tomas Hintnaus, who holds Brazil's record and formerly held it for all of South America (18–10½, or 5.75), competed while wearing a strip of rawhide, knotted into a bracelet. The coiled bracelet was as long as the distance between his personal best and Bubka's world record. Hintnaus said the twist of leather showed him how small a difference there was between being good and being the best. What it really showed, however, was the gap between every other pole-vaulter and the limits of human performance. The sky really was the limit with Bubka.

He always dominates discussions when pole-vaulters gather. What did he know that the others didn't? He ran to the box as they did, although perhaps faster, and he planted as they did, although perhaps harder, and then he soared above their dream jumps. Yet his defeats and disappointments kept him human. He is the reference point that fixes our concept of the pole vault. He is as important to the sport as the knots are that secure the threads in a tapestry. His name is synonymous with flying in the way Ruth is synonymous with power. Like only a very few of the very best, Bubka is part of the very DNA of his sport.

8 "Crash" Course

Toby "Crash" Stevenson dominated the first half of the Olympic year of 2004 like skyrockets dominate the sky on the Fourth of July. He was jumping big and flying high. He would charge the sky and overwhelm it just like Bubka.

If he wasn't Bubka, he was still a strummin', struttin' spectacular, letting it all go when he came down from the top of his world. Sometimes, he rode the pole through the pits like Happy Gilmore, doing the bull dance, feeling the flow. Sometimes, he did the "Robot," walking mechanically like a *Star Wars* android gone clear across the galaxy and back. Sometimes, he turned the pole into an air guitar, and the fans could catch the vibe—Jimi Hendrix in "Purple Haze" wailing, "'Scuse me, while I kiss the sky."

It was a season of crescendos and competitive clarity for him. Toby Stevenson had seen the glory of the event and had breathed the same air as the sport's legends. He had come to Sacramento for the 2004 U.S. Olympic Trials as the best jumper in the world. On May 8, in Modesto, California, he had PR'd three times in one afternoon, adding an astonishing 10 inches to his personal record. The last height was 19–8¼, the fabled six-meter mark, which in pole vaulting is the threshold of legend. "It was a real breakthrough, a lot of things coming together," Stevenson said. "When I woke up that day, I knew I was going to jump high, I just didn't know how high. I wanted to jump 5.90 [meters, 19–4¼], and six meters was just the icing."

It had been easy. It had been the fulfillment of the mystical, contradictory concept of effortless power. It's a concept that spans many sports. Baseball players seldom hit home runs when they are trying to. The best drives in golf are pure and chaste, kissed by the sweet spot, not grip-it and rip-it exertions. The best pole vaults are Rocky, once he got in shape, running the Art Museum steps in Philadelphia as if they were a stairway to heaven. Gonna fly now.

"It was what every athlete wishes for," Stevenson said. "Whenever you do a really good jump, it looks easy. The six-meter jump was the easiest jump of my life. I hit it just right."

Stevenson tried to reconstruct it, but he couldn't. The prophet Elijah said mankind only gets a glimpse of the hem of God's garments. Pole-vaulters seldom see more than a stitch or two.

Veteran pole-vaulter Pat Manson, who cleared 18 feet every year for twenty-one straight years, is a man who should know about meeting the demands of the event. "A perfect jump," he said, "is like doing a perfect golf swing in the middle of a long jump. There are maybe fifty things that have to go right to make the perfect jump. The world's very best vaulters do maybe thirty-five of those right, forty at most. You do forty, and it's a career day. Every vaulter gets a glimpse of it, and that's what keeps you trying to do it again."

"It's over so soon, you can't really savor it," Stevenson said of the experience. "You release with more energy than the pole has. It's a feeling of weightlessness. When it happens, you don't even see the crossbar to worm over it. You see the crossbar, and then you're over it."

"Crash" Stevenson was going over bars as nimbly as a bouncer ready to give the heave-ho to a troublemaker. He went to the Trials as the overwhelming favorite. He won his first five meets of the year. Modesto was a validation of half his life and more, years and years of topsy-turvy soaring.

Stevenson started pole-vaulting in the seventh grade, at the age of twelve. His father, Eddy, had been a 14-foot pole-vaulter in college in the 1960s, a respectable height in that era. Eddy built his son a pole vault pit in the backyard, consisting of a 100-foot-long raised wooden runway, standards, mattresses, and foam rubber they had collected around the hot, dusty West Texas town of Odessa. "You don't buy a pre-fab kit; you have to use some ingenuity to make a pole vault pit," Stevenson said.

While Eddy had been a skydiver, Toby, a hell-for-leather street-bike racer as a kid, was expected to use a little more restraint. To please his mother, he vaulted in a roller hockey crash helmet. Hence, the nickname "Crash." Given his exuberance after clearances, another nickname for Stevenson, "The Cat in the Hat," seemed equally appropriate. Said the Dr. Seuss character, shortly before falling in a stunt and landing on his head: "Look at me! Look at me now! It is fun to have fun. But you have to know how."

"Odessa is flat and brown, but it's a really good place to grow up," Stevenson said. "I was always in gymnastics. I was a gymnast when my dad put up the pole vault pit. The first day, I jumped about sixty times. The next morning, I couldn't get out of bed."

Odessa received national attention with the publication of *Friday Night Lights,* a book that chronicled the town's high school football obsession. It's a town that was down on its luck when the oil patch went bust in the 1980s. *Friday Night Lights* turned it into a symbol of any community committed too devoutly to athletic excellence.

Stevenson, like any top pole-vaulter, was a marvel of coordination. But by the time he might have caught the eye of the football coach, he was well past the starting age. His PR in high school was 17 feet, enough for Stanford to offer him a scholarship. Anyone who goes to school in golden California carries the aura of it with him like the radiance around a saint's head in a Renaissance painting. In the cold, dark East, watching events such as the Rose Bowl in California made other Americans, because of the three-hour time difference, think of it as a land of perpetual light, a mellow place about which the Beach Boys and Jan and Dean sang. There, the surf was always up, two girls were always available for every guy, and the latest always arrived early.

Like most generalizations, it wasn't especially true. Stevenson did have some of the "every day is a nice day" West Coast outlook, but he was a Texan at heart. Maybe only Texas was big enough to contain his emotional surges, which would geyser out after a big clearance and make the oil gusher in which James Dean frolicked in the quintessential Texas movie *Giant* look weak and half-assed.

"I have always seen myself as a Texan," he said. "Every state has a lot of pride, but Texas has a little more. Texas has such a great history. Everybody knows 'Remember the Alamo.' And it's such a big state, with so many people. Wherever you are in the world, you have a better chance of meeting someone from Texas than, say, from Rhode Island."

"Weather, geography, climate—Texans just have a little more of everything," Stevenson continued. "You can find anything you want there."

In a state whose present was formed by a past that included Indian wars, cattle drives, and the law of the gun, he was a space cowboy. Records? Bring 'em on!

Improvement can come like lightning striking. It had in Modesto. It could again.

Everything Stevenson did was designed, Bubka-like, to make him stronger. "I don't think there are any big secrets in the pole vault," Stevenson said. "I don't do very trendy training. It's very boring. I work my ass off when I'm in the weight room. I work my ass off when I'm doing speed work."

Pigeonholing Mack and Stevenson is unfair to either. But if you had to say which aspect of Bubka each most copied, it would have been brains with Mack, brawn with Stevenson.

Stevenson might not go parasailing or hang-gliding on the day of meets to relax, a daredevil regimen adopted by the American vaulter Tye Harvey, but he enjoyed his success. He would clear a bar and come down bellowing, and then he would be dancing, rapturous, a man who had seen Paradise.

Bob Richards, for his part, was a showman. "I like that emotion Stevenson brings to it," he said.

Charmingly, Stevenson was not just a Texan full of tall tales and taller jumps, but he had a self-deprecating nature. The pole-vaulter's common misfortune had happened to the Cat in the Hat—walking out of the pit after a successful jump, catching a spike in the pads and face-planting! It does wonders in counteracting ego.

Mack was much more Bubka's disciple in terms of self-containment. For example, Stevenson and fellow Californian Derek Miles were always talking at meets in a public display of gregariousness. Mack, the man who didn't say much, was always private.

"I'm not out to psych out a guy. I'm in my own little world," Mack said. "For me, not saying anything to the other guys is almost a psych.

I'm not talking at all, and they know I'm focused completely on what I have to do. A lot of guys are talkers. Guys like that, it relaxes them. If you don't talk, they don't know how to react."

Mack isn't rude, but he burrows into that tunnel where the vaulting cues are stashed, and hoards his energy there. He might as well be Bubka, paring down unnecessary emotions just as the market cheat whittled down the small wedge of cheese when Sergey was a boy. He might as well be Seagren, unaware of the civil rights protest on the victory stand at the 1968 Olympics because he had a world-record bar to challenge.

Bubka, however, would go over the bar with a banshee yell. At meets, "What's up?" is enough small talk for Mack.

Of his celebrations, Stevenson said: "It's not real craziness. But we are a professional sport. The crowd is a huge part of the event. Any pole-vaulter will tell you that. I want the crowd to be totally excited when I'm out there. If they see this guy going crazy after clearing a bar, they might tell their friends, and they all might come out the next time. I see it as helping the sport, helping other pole-vaulters."

"Crash" is an inch shorter than Mack at 6–1, but he weighs ten more pounds. More bulk in a smaller package gives him a more strapping appearance. With his mane of dark hair, his helmet, and his chin "patch," Stevenson is the most recognizable figure in the event. With his theatrics, he is also the most flamboyant. By contrast, with his face an iron mask, with every extraneous emotion shorn off like his ruthless haircuts, Mack doesn't give anything about himself away cheaply. Restraint isn't a prison for Mack; it's a weapon.

"Toby was jumping pretty high early in high school. I wasn't," said Mack. "But you compete against the event itself—all the years that have gone into trying to master the pole vault, all the emotion you have invested. Over a competition, what Toby does is a lot of energy to expend. At the end, if you have spent even 1 percent of your energy on that, it might be what it takes to clear the bar. My attitude to Toby is, 'Fine. Waste that energy.'"

Mack is the reluctant daredevil, the freethinker who devised a stouter lance, the outsider over whom few schools fought. He was convinced three years out that 2004 was his year. Nothing was going to detract from the skill and will it took to get over the bar. He would conserve his resources, hoard his energy. They wouldn't know what hit them.

"I'm not a selfish person," said Mack. "But it's all about me at a competition. I'm really selfish then. I never minded being out of the spotlight. It isn't about having fun. I want to jump as high as I can, make money at it, and compete. That's what guides me. My energy goes into jumping higher."

Stevenson had been the best jumper in the world in the first half of 2004. Still, he knew what Miles had thought in the Jonesboro, Arkansas, pre-Trials meet of the onrushing Mack. "Whoa. Whole new jumper!" Miles had said as Mack nearly scraped over six meters.

The whole new jumper had made his promise to himself of Goldnathens. Now, he was back in the same city where he had failed four years earlier, back in Sacramento. Mack was about to show he could fulfill his secret, glittering pledge.

The capital of California, Sacramento is a city without Los Angeles' Beverly Hills chic or Hollywood sign, without San Francisco's little cable cars climbing halfway to the stars, without Oakland's piratical Raiders and "Just win, baby" ethos, even without San Diego's zoo.

By bidding on and winning the Olympic Trials in 2000 and 2004, Sacramento sought to establish a reputation as a track hotbed. In terms of track interest, record numbers of tickets were sold to Sacramento State's Hornet Stadium in 2000. In terms of being, literally, a hotbed, it also reached its goal. In the summer, Sacramento is hot and dry. The "Delta" wind, so named because its origin is over the delta of the Sacramento River, seldom blew during the 2000 Trials. The heat reached the nineties regularly. It wasn't as hot in 2004, but the sun, the dust, and the smoke from the pit fires of the concession area barbecues still gave it the feel of a meet Lucifer would have loved.

The stadium, courtesy of a $1 million renovation financed by San Diego Chargers owner and Sacramento businessman Alex G. Spanos, was the site of the 2003 NCAA Track and Field Championships. After a pause in 2004 for the University of Texas to stage the event, Sacramento became the host for the collegiate championships the next three years. In some ways, this is typical of the shortsightedness of the people who run track and field in the United States. The time difference ruthlessly curtails the ability of Eastern and Central Time Zone newspapers to cover the event. *Track and Field News* also complained that Hornet Stadium was "antiquated," despite the makeover, with "horrid sightlines."

Perhaps no one can actively discourage interest in track and field more energetically than the people in charge of it. There were two "rest days" during the eleven days of the 2004 Trials, to drag the Trials out for two weekends and expand network television coverage.

Nike used the first rest day, July 13, to unveil the official Swoosher-ized, streamlined, body-hugging, cutting-edge USA uniforms, supplied by, ahem, you-know-whom. USA Track and Field publicist Jill Geer introduced the runners and jumpers. While Mack wasn't one of the models, Mack's girlfriend, Grace Upshaw, one of the most photogenic track and field athletes, was there. Toby Stevenson also posed on the stage. The choice of a pole vaulter was, according to longtime coach Greg Hull, a no-brainer. "Pole vaulters tend to be physically attractive men and women. They have wide shoulders, narrow hips, and they're tall, lean and muscled," he said.

Dozens of track and field writers, scrounging for angles on a fallow day, showed up at the modeling session. Many hoped for interview opportunities beyond the fashion do's and don'ts, although such questions were discouraged and discussion instead centered on fashion. Other reporters attempted irreverence. But in the technogeek sport of track and field, many reporters were perfectly happy to explain why Nike apparel was just another weapon in Uncle Sam's ensemble.

Knights fitted with armor plates weren't tended to any more meticulously, it seems. Mack, the battered and bloodied knight, would have appreciated Nike's "armoring" efforts. He had watched *A Knight's Tale* time and again because he identified so closely with Will Thatcher, the "half-starved scarecrow with lots of spirit," who dubbed himself Ulrich von Liechtenstein.

Media attendance, embarrassingly, was far less on the next rest day, when Sacramento's Chamber of Commerce brought some of the greatest track and field athletes in the country's history to the convention center downtown. Sacramento knows how to revive memories. Old Sacramento is a 28-acre area of historic buildings restored to the way they were in the Gold Rush days. The early days are reflected in the wooden sidewalks, horse-drawn carriages, and Mississippi-style riverboats. It was only a few blocks from "Old Sac" with its steam engines and one-room schoolhouse to the convention center. But the men and women who made track and field history were only an afterthought to those in charge of the sport today.

Bob Beamon, who jumped over the boundaries of what was possible; Bob Mathias, twice the Olympic decathlon gold medalist, the first time at the age of seventeen; Jackie Joyner-Kersee, the greatest female track and field athlete since Babe Didriksen; the Tennessee State Tiger Belles, featuring Madeline Manning, who dominated Olympic track when racism and sexism could have held them down—no one who loved track and field would have stayed away.

But Nike had no stake in it, and the official USATF media guide barely mentioned it. As about thirty writers roamed between the tables in the cavernous second-floor ballroom, visiting those stirring yesterdays, you had to wonder: How can America nurture future track and field stars, when its nature is to ignore the most glorious names of the sport's past?

Americans who make it through the Trials have already been through an almost Darwinian selection process. Any of ten men could have gone to Athens at the 2004 Trials. Only three would. All of the sky-jumpers knew that.

In the American system, there's no reserving a place on the team for a dominant track and field athlete who picks the worst time of the year to get injured or fall ill. No spot was held for the great sprinter Carl Lewis, when he was sick at the Trials in 1996 and was lucky to make the team as a long jumper and nothing else.

There's no provision made for the inexplicable screwup, such as when decathlete Dan O'Brien no-heighted his opening bar, set at 15–9, in the 1992 Trials. That was the most shocking example ever of the pole vault as a disaster event. A jump of 12 feet would have put O'Brien on the team in Barcelona. Instead, he stayed behind. In subsequent decathlons, he made his first jump at 15–1 to make sure he got a mark in. "I can practically sit over that [15–1] bar," he said.

So high were the stakes that the deeply religious Macks went to mass at the towering Cathedral of the Blessed Sacrament each morning when Tim competed. Candles they had left burning shed a soft light, as they prayed for God to guide him to his best efforts. A friend of his mother's had also asked the nuns at Our Lady of Victory in Lackawanna, New York, the friend's hometown, to pray the rosary for Mack.

Ten Americans had cleared 5.80 meters (19–0¼) going into the 2004 Trials. No 19-foot pole-vaulter at the Trials had ever failed to make an Olympic team. But there is a first time for everything.

In the lead-up to the Trials, Bemiller, ever encouraging, tried some psychological reinforcement on Mack. When they would talk, Bemiller would say: "See ya later, Champ."

"Oh, my God. Did he just call me 'Champ?'" Mack said the first time it happened.

Psychologists call this "Pygmalion therapy," after the Shaw play that was the basis for the musical *My Fair Lady.* The idea is that a teacher's (or coach's) expectations about a person eventually lead the person to behavior that confirms the expectations. Call a man a champ, and he'll be a champ—provided he puts in the 10,000 hours of work Bob Richards advised as complements to a daily bowl of Wheaties.

Every stadium offers its own peculiarities. Hornet Stadium, with its 22,000-seat capacity, the largest in the NCAA's Big Sky Conference, was no different. Reporters reached the main press box and the auxiliary one on its roof via an antiquated elevator run by an operator who swung the dungeon-like gate shut. In the heat, different operators came on every few hours. It was sweltering in the tiny oven-like contraption. Dust stirred in the burning wind. The setting sun glared on computer screens in the rooftop press box. Daily journalism is frontline stuff, but in the aerie atop the sun-baked stadium, it felt like being a cat on a hot tin roof.

For competitors, it was even tougher. "It's a difficult venue. It's a low stadium, open-ended. The wind gets in there and swirls around. You don't get a nice tailwind every time," said Bemiller. "It has variable winds, usually a crosswind, right to left. The runway is also on a crown [the rise in the field that allows water to drain]. A lot of runways in the United States are on the straightaways. Running on the crown can throw your stride off. You run up the crown, and then you come back down it. You push a little harder with your stride going out, and you're a little bit out of position the second half of your run."

Jeff Hartwig knew about being out of position. It was getting to be an old story for him in Sacramento. "There are always certain people you expect to do well," said Stevenson. "But that's the beauty/frustration of the pole vault. Anything can happen. Look at Hartwig."

"If you need proof of how tough the wind is, Mr. Hartwig could attest to that. Twice," said Bemiller.

Pole vault qualifying was the first day of the Trials. Hartwig—who had perched on the stack of sticks as the chartered plane droned to Bubka's meet in Donetsk, who had gone higher than any American ever when he jumped 19–9½ (6.03) in 2000—would be gone almost before the meet began.

It was a bumpy landing. But he was getting used to that in Sacramento. He had also no-heighted in Sacramento in 2000. The thirty-six-year-old Hartwig came to Sacramento knowing it was probably his last chance at an Olympic medal. They begin as boys, going where eagles dare, as sunshine jumpers up on the roof. At the end of the day, not even the highest-flying of them are guaranteed the splendor of sunset.

Hartwig had jumped all the way to the shrine of pole vaulting in Bubka's hometown. In Sacramento on July 9, he missed all three tries at 5.50 meters, or 18–0½ (four, actually, since he was given an additional vault after winning a protest). The American eagle had landed with a thud.

An official red-flagged Hartwig for taking too long on his third attempt. Jumpers have one minute after the bar is set in qualifying to make an attempt. The fickle winds picked up as Hartwig began his last run, and then it became an agony of indecision. It's what every competitor fears, flying by the seat of his pants, unable to get his bearings. It's why Mack built a support system of numbers. It's one of the most difficult things to do in one of the most difficult disciplines in sports, changing poles and strategies while on the clock. Indecision put the bar too high even for Bubka on his no-height in Barcelona. There are no odds high enough against clearing a bar in such circumstances.

"On my third attempt, I stopped short because the wind hit me," said Hartwig. "As I started back to restart my run, I asked how much time was left, and I was told twelve seconds. I ran back to the end of the runway and grabbed a different pole, because I was tired. As I picked up the pole, the official at the pit raised the red flag."

Hartwig protested that the marks he had placed to direct his route had been moved. The protest was upheld. But when, twenty minutes after the qualifying ostensibly ended, he took his do-over, he knocked the bar off again.

"My heart went out to him," said Stevenson. "But am I relieved he's out? Yeah, I am."

Mack was surprised Hartwig got another chance. "At that point, I don't think it made much difference for Hartwig," he said. "The fact that Hartwig was out increased my chances. I hated it for him, but my margin of error went up."

They dream of flight. But when you are as old as Hartwig in Sacramento, Icarus falls hard.

Lawrence Johnson also no-heighted. Four years after the Olympic silver medal; after winning the U.S. Trials in 1996 and 2000; after being dubbed the best black pole-vaulter there ever was; after being the University of Tennessee pole-vaulter who always overshadowed Mack; after years of breaking down barriers; after all that, Lawrence Johnson had failed to clear the 18-foot bar. To increase his speed, Johnson trained with controversial coach John Smith of HSI Sports. HSI sprinter Mickey Grimes received a two-year ban after testing positive for steroids from USADA in 2004, while two other HSI sprinters, Torri Edwards and Larry Wade, also drew drug-related suspensions.

Only the injury potential of pole vaulting kept LoJo from perhaps becoming the Tiger Woods of the event and changing the parameters of what was possible. You're going to get punished in the pole vault, because it's not just rare air and the zero-gravity convergences of a perfect vault; it's a hit pit, just as running a pass route over the middle in the NFL is a collision curriculum. But sometimes, a man has just taken too many hits. That is likely what happened to LoJo in Sacramento. "He didn't have any kind of base," said Bemiller. "He was banged up in the ankle and the shoulder. He needed a year off to get healthy. He also has other demands on his time now. He was married with two kids."

The top-ranked collegiate pole-vaulter, Tommy Skipper of Oregon, also no-heighted despite a re-vault. Skipper had a glittering record that made him a name to watch—national high school record holder as a junior at 17–8 and a senior at 18–3, *Track and Field News* High School Athlete of the Year, Pac-10 pole vault and decathlon champion, the latter in his first-ever decathlon. Still, Mack saw in Skipper a flashback to himself in Atlanta—unable to adapt, doomed in the struggle to get over the bar.

"There was a strong wind from the right side," Mack said. "You don't go into qualifying to try to win it. So, in the wind, I changed poles. I wanted to use the softest pole possible. I was prepared, and I didn't want to mess around. But he [Skipper] never adjusted."

As for Mack, he hit his one jump at the qualifying standard perfectly. The muscle he had gained since 2000 in the weight room, sweat droplet by sweat droplet until they became rivulets and then skin-slicking, shirt-plastering torrents, gave him the strength to fight the wind. Ten others also qualified.

It isn't necessary to win the Trials. You just have to finish in the top three to make the Olympic team. In the final, Tim Mack would have to make the team or miss it on one jump that put at risk the dreams of more than half his life.

Track and field possesses a terrible yet satisfying objectivity. "At least," said Bragg, "I didn't have to kiss up to any judge as a pole-vaulter. I'd never have made it in a subjective sport."

A scoring error in the men's all-around gymnastics final in Athens threw the gold medal into the hands of lawyers, and the case went all the way to the Court of Arbitration for Sport before American Paul Hamm got to keep what he had won in the arena. Biased judges have denied boxers their due too, most notably Roy Jones Jr., who used a South Korean's head as a speed bag in 1988 yet lost to home cooking, prepared by the judges in Seoul.

No such uncertainty attends track and field. It is scrupulously timed and carefully measured. For that very reason, track and field is also spared the Golden Age yearnings of other sports.

Team USA in men's basketball in Athens was considered by purists to be an insult to its illustrious predecessors. But you never find anyone arguing that Jesse Owens could run faster than Athens 100-meter gold medalist and former University of Tennessee sprinter Justin Gatlin. There are always anomalies, like Florence Griffith Joyner and Bubka, with all their baggage of drug suspicion in the 1988 Olympics. But in many ways, these are the good old days. No one is trained to such a pitch of readiness, with such expert coaching, such nutritional exactness, such computerized feedback and, undeniably in a few cases, such chemical enhancement as track and field athletes today. In a world in which not even the 2000 American presidential election was resolved at the ballot box, but rather in the courts; in a time in which America has fragmented into quarrelsome red and blue enclaves; in an atmosphere of suspicion and distrust for the electoral process and constitutional guarantees, track and field offers finality. Citius, fortius, altius. Firstest gets the mostest. Highest touches the stars.

Mack, of course, came to the Trials to win. Anything else would represent a compromise, a betrayal of the work ethic that had fueled him for so long. He was becoming a great clutch pole-vaulter precisely because he never took it for granted, always worked for what he got, never had it made, always had to stay with it, and never forgot that genius and talent are dust under the wheel of persistence.

The Trials were a preview of Athens. The biggest jump of his life until Athens had nothing in it of Bragg's "picture this" perfection. No flashbulb blazed in his head. There was nothing of rope swings or tree houses to it. There was nothing of effortlessness, no analogy to sending the little white, dimpled ball streaking out there like a flash of light, right down the middle of the fairway. There was nothing of the Lost Boys either, unless it was the immaturity Mack had shed over so many years of competing.

When Tim Mack jumped onto the Olympic team on the afternoon of July 11 in Sacramento, he went through turbulence. He fought for every inch of lift. He never backed down even though elements of the jump were unsynchronized. He never once considered aborting it. He made the jump work. He hit back. He fought his way to the stars like the martial angels of John Milton in *Paradise Lost*.

The final at the Trials was a spectacular enough competition as it was, with four men jumping 19 feet. Even more, it displayed all the factors that make it such a compelling event—clutch clearances, height enough to make a groundling's head swim, the first-ever 19-foot jumper (Tye Harvey) who stayed home, and tactical maneuvers that made it seem like airborne chess. In such a contest, you go with the knight who had been through the most jousts with the bar.

Passing after a miss is a gambit that introduces a new hazard. The miss carries over to the next height and reduces the competitor's complement of attempts. At the Trials, there were more passes in the pole vault final than in the singles bars around town.

Russ Buller, who had trained with LoJo while Mack drilled alone at Tennessee, passed first after missing once at 18–4½ (5.60 meters). At 18–8¼ (5.70), Miles and Mack cleared on their first attempts. The two thirty-one-year-olds were tied for first. Harvey scraped over at the height on his third try. Buller, who would pass thirteen times in all, wriggled over it, too. But then Jim Davis, using the passing strategy, sailed over at 18–10¼ (5.75). At 19–0¼ [5.80], four vaulters missed once then passed. One of them was Mack. This forced him to make a critical decision.

"Toby, Miles and Harvey had all made 5.80," said Mack. "It did me no good to jump at it. If I cleared, all it meant was I would have three tries at 19–2¼ [5.85], not two. I didn't need attempts. I needed to clear a bar before anyone else."

"He was in first place at 18–8," Bemiller said. "We said we'd see what happens. He missed his first jump at 19 feet, and too many other guys had cleared. It was a worthless jump. I was proud of him. He never thought twice about passing. The problem was not height that day. The problem was getting off the ground cleanly."

Bemiller was standing near the fourth turn of the oval, on the same fence in the same stadium where he had stood in 2000 when Mack flamed out and kicked the bar off going up in the final. Bemiller's blood was up. Perhaps he undervalued how daunting 19–2¼ was. "I was thinking about everything [in the jump] being in the right place and being aggressive. But that height would have gotten you a bronze medal in Athens. I should have been more nervous about it," he said.

Miles now was first with no misses through 19–2¼. Stevenson was second at the same height, but he had missed once at 18–8¼ and then cleared. Third was Harvey, who made the one attempt he had left after passing a good one.

Mack, with a best bar of 18–8¼, missed on the first of his two tries at 19–2¼. He was in seventh place with one jump left. It was Eminem's one shot, one opportunity to seize everything he wanted. One try to go from peasant to knight, from toilets to the torch.

"So much was riding on that next jump," said Tim O'Hare, who was signaling wind direction to Tim in the stands. "I felt the pressure as a fan and a friend. I thought, 'Oh, no. He's been jumping 19–4 for three weeks!'"

"Oh, my God! I could be out," Mack thought as he faced the bar at 19–2¼ for his last attempt.

Then he said: "The hell with that. I am going to do everything I had learned over a lot of years to give myself a shot. I have been planning this for years."

Mack looked into the stands and found Tim O'Hare, who gave him an urgent wave. The signal meant he had a tailwind: the pole-vaulter's friend.

"It's okay to be behind, as long as you're not pressing or stressing," Mack said. "Perseverance is what I do."

The jumping cues were all he was thinking about. Keep your posture. Work your arms. "The Book" had banished mental doubts. "I knew I was on the right pole. I knew the standards were right. It came down to a matter of will," said Mack.

As Mack began to run, "B," craning his neck from the fence, saw that his pupil had missed his mark at the midpoint. When you're running for your life's dream, cads might as well be chasing you. All the scripted choreography can become garble. You run as if everything depends on it, because it does.

"He was one foot inside his mark at the midpoint, but I thought he was okay. He wasn't leaning or falling forward on the run," said Bemiller. "He should have hit the mark at 54 feet, 6 inches, but he was a foot inside."

No turning back now, "B" thought. "You've got to go!" the voice inside Bemiller's head was screaming, as the crowd rose all around him, roaring. "A lot of vaulters get too close to the box, and they'll brake or not push on the pole," the coach said. "But Tim had to go, no matter what. It was his worst inside step of the day and worst takeoff. But he attacked with his arms and kept his posture."

"My body was making adjustments in the air," Mack said. "It was like going the wrong way in a car. You're on some side streets, and you've got to get back on path. You don't take the main streets, and you can't stop for directions at the 7-Eleven."

Mack went over the bar like an upside-down limbo dancer, wriggling and writhing. He brushed it with the jersey on his chest, no harder than the flutter of an angel's wing.

"I knew I didn't hit it hard enough to knock it off. You know it when you've done that," said Mack.

"It was bouncing around a little bit," worried Bemiller.

When the quivering died away to a twitch and then to a tic and then to stillness, Mack pumped his fist triumphantly. For just one instant, the knight could raise his visor. The rigid control could unbend just a bit. For an eye-blink, Tim had become Toby, jubilant in the pit. He came out of the pads like the cork comes out of a bottle of champagne.

Miles missed three times at 19–2¼ and would be going to Athens as the third man on the team on fewer misses over Harvey. The reigning Olympic champion, Hysong, was out at 19–2¼ too. So both Sydney medalists, Hysong and Johnson, were gone. Hartwig, the American record holder, was gone. At the Trials, history is something you make, not something you can lean on for support.

First place now was up to Mack or Stevenson, and Mack—the pressure off, the team made—busted his best jump in Sacramento, skying over the bar at 19-4¼ like a jet contrail.

"He was on the team, so he was living it up, being aggressive. He was way over it," said Bemiller.

Bemiller and other coaches thought that jump, on which Mack had about 10 centimeters (four inches) of clearance, was one of the best jumps, attained with the most blinding swing speed, that they ever saw.

On his second and last attempt, "Crash" was over the bar by so much he could have had on landing gear and retractable wings, but he thumped it on the way down.

"Oh, you're good. You're really good," Mack's mother later told the friend from western New York who had asked the nuns to pray.

In the pole vault, it isn't over even when it's over. You always do an encore, always play another set, always take a final bow. "There are two constants about the pole vault," said Russ Johnson, Mack's old University of Tennessee roommate. "There's no doubt whether you succeed or not. But you always end on a miss."

So they set the bar almost a half-foot higher at an American record, 19-9¾ (6.04). Mack's first two tries were very close. Asked how close he had come, Mack said: "Close enough to make it next time."

The victory meant he would go to his first Olympics as a better-known underdog, a journeyman who had brushed the bar but would get to fly on toward the sun. The golden dream he had lived with every time he turned on his computer was close enough to touch.

Mack, Stevenson, and Miles took the victory lap in Hornet Stadium, each holding a portion of a giant American flag. Mack's hand was on the striped end. In so many ways, however, he had reached the unreachable star.

9 Dreams

It's gotta be the shoes? Bemiller wouldn't swear by the theory advanced by Spike Lee in Michael Jordan's early Nike commercials, but he was taking no chances. On the day of the pole vault final at the Athens Olympics, "B" caught the Metro, riding the train as it rumbled down toward the Plaka, the oldest residential area in the city. This time, he knew the way. The old agora of ancient times, the city's marketplace, is huddled to one side of the Plaka. Above it is the Acropolis, crowned with the marble monuments that were the glory of the ancient world. Nearby is the Temple of Theseus.

For his part, Bemiller wasn't one to ignore a routine that had previously worked. He had made this same trip two days earlier when Mack had qualified for the final, although not without duress. "I went the first time for shoes. I went the second time for karma," the coach said.

On August 25, prelims day, Bemiller, wearing a vivid, floral-printed shirt that made him look like a man late for a luau, prowled the Monistiraki Flea Market. Finally, after wandering through a maze of narrow alleys, he found the shop of Stavros Melissinos, "The Poet Sandal Maker."

It is a small, dark, and cluttered place. Most of the storefront is devoted to photographs and news clips featuring Melissinos and famous people. John Lennon had been an early fan, and he brought the rest of the Beatles to the shop. Jackie Onassis, Rudolph Nureyev, Sophia Loren, and Gregory Peck were other customers.

While Melinissos has remained a cobbler all his life, his poetry is highly esteemed in Europe and is taught in British universities. Melissinos once wrote:

Take away the Glories and the Honors
The granite palaces of this vain World
And only give me the Smile of Pain, the Tear of Joy
And I will erect a thousand palaces in me in which to live

Greece was not a dusty museum that can only preserve the past, the poem said. In Greece, life was intense and deeply felt. The emotions poured out like the heady wine from Zorba's goatskin.

The truth of the assertion was not hard to find. "Hel-las! Hel-las!" the Greeks chanted whenever a countryman or woman won a medal. "Greece! Greece!" In the preliminaries, Bemiller and Mack found that the nation could pass for an outdoor madhouse on a jubilation bender.

After Bemiller had bought sandals for his daughters Gracie and Kelsey and his wife Missy, he discovered he was running too late to return to his apartment and change for the qualifying. So he showed up with the dust from the Plaka on his skin and the *Hawaii Five-o* shirt on his back.

Some coaches subscribe to a general theory that under Olympic pressure one-third of the field will not reach the level of performance that got them to the competition; one-third will equal that level; and one-third will exceed it. And so qualifying, just as in the U.S. Trials, was filled with unpleasant surprises for big names.

Five men at the Athens qualifying had jumped six meters—Stevenson; Dmitri Markov, now jumping for Australia; the German pair of Tim Lobinger and Danny Ecker; and South Africa's Okert Brits. Mack would cross the threshold of greatness shortly after the Olympics. Australia's Paul Burgess would do so in 2005. That meant half of the fourteen men in all of history who would clear the golden bar were competing in Athens. It was truly a conclave in the clouds.

Markov didn't even make it far enough to challenge the automatic qualifying (AQ) mark of 5.70 meters, or 18–8¼. He missed at 5.65 meters, or 18–6½. Only Bubka had ever jumped higher than Markov, but now Markov was gone in a fiery plunge.

France's Romain Mesnil, a 19-foot man in 2004, like Markov, scraped over on his third try at 18–6½ but missed the AQ mark. Brits, who had jumped 18–10¼ earlier in the year, couldn't clear either.

Mack, after easily making 18–0½ and 18–4½, passed until the AQ mark. But before he could make his first attempt, Athens native Fani Halkia raced out of the night like a goddess from Mount Olympus, descending to slum around with the mortals. Fresh from an Olympic record in the semifinals, Halkia stormed to victory in the women's 400-meter hurdles minutes before Mack was to jump. It was Greece's first gold medal in track and field, and the party-hearty Athenians' dancing shoes were on. The wild music from *Zorba the Greek* rose to a mad pitch, louder even than the exultant roar of the 72,000 in Olympic Stadium. The mandolin-like instrument making the frenetic music was called a bouzouki. The bouzouki bazooka-ed. The crowd chanted "Hel-las! Hel-las!" Blue and white Greek flags flew in the stands as Halkia took a victory lap that would have gotten Terrell Owens, Joe Horn, Randy Moss and every other dancin' machine in the NFL a penalty for excessive celebration. "Hel-las! Hel-las!" rang out. It went on and on, a tear of joy that glistened in every eye in Greece.

Hours later, weary journalists, returning at 5 A.M. to their college dormitory–style rooms, would get only cursory security checks from the normally grim-faced Greek Army soldiers stationed at the gates with automatic rifles slung over their shoulders. "We won!" shouted one soldier with a smile like daybreak lighting his face. "Hel-las! Hel-las!"

Tim Mack had been an outsider at the party for years until his skills gradually increased. Now he was on the runway, readying for his qualifying jump, the most important moment of his life to that point, and Halkia's gold had reduced him to the very definition of the word "inconsequential." The riot of sound swept all Mack's rigid control and iron discipline away. Halkia, a Greek flag in her hands, was rounding the curve near the pole vault pit when Mack, who was on the clock, started to run toward the vault box. "Hel-las! Hel-las!"

A feather had a better chance of riding out a tornado. "It went on and on," said Mack. "I had jumped 6 inches higher than that bar, but the Greek girl won the hurdles, and then it was the all-time party."

Tim O'Hare, who had spent $2,400 of his own money to fly to the meet and scout the wind for Mack, stood in the stands above Bemiller, stunned by the deafening ovation. "It was my first international meet. I felt I was at Neyland Stadium in Knoxville at a big football game," he said. The colossal stadium on the banks of the Tennessee River has a listed capacity of 104,079.

Mack, visibly flustered, missed badly. "I ran differently, rushed and missed. I got too caught up in it. I was mad that I allowed myself to get caught up in the surroundings," said Mack. "It was a lesson learned."

On his second attempt, Mack cleared easily enough for it to have been just another day at the altitude office. He bagged his poles then walked slowly over to where Bemiller was sitting. Mack took in the "Where's the roast suckling pig?" attire of his coach. "Don't wear your beach shirt to the final," Mack said.

In Greece, history was literally underfoot. One of the reasons the Greek organizers barely beat the IOC's deadline on building competitive venues was the archeological prizes the backhoes and bulldozers kept unearthing. Greece invented organized sports. The Greeks were the first people to play, which said much for the quality of life they established. As classical scholar Edith Hamilton famously observed, a people burdened by toil, narrowed by religious proscriptions, and cowed by fear does not play. The Greeks did.

The greatest sports festival of the ancient Greeks was held in Olympia in western Greece in a valley green as springtime despite the summer heat. Three other great festivals were held in other parts of Greece. A truce was declared for the quadrennial Olympics in the ancient world, one that protected spectators and participants traveling to Olympia.

The men's and women's shot put competition was held at Olympia in 2004. It was a master stroke. The Greeks returned the Olympics to the ground in Olympia where organized sports began in the world. And they did so in the least intrusive way, for the shot put requires only about a 75-foot-long playing field. It was a four-and-a-half-hour bus ride from Athens for those who traveled there to report on it. The distances must have been absolutely staggering in the ancient world when the methods of getting there included sandal power, rowed galleys, and swingin' low in your sweet chariot.

Almost every modern competitor—in Athens if he was not lucky enough to have gone to Olympia—channeled some of the spirit of the old Greeks. It was a corny ideal, especially with the Summer Games grown into a sporting lollapalooza listing teams from 202 countries and with the drug scandal clouding track and field. Still, in Athens, and particularly in Olympia, you checked your cynicism at the admission gate. The impractical, unlikely, and inextinguishable ideal was that people from different places with different customs could meet in peaceful contests and find in their common aspirations unity and equality.

Rivers gorged with snowmelt from distant mountains made Olympia an oasis in the searing heat. This, you came to understand, was how sports worked too. For all their drawbacks, they irrigate our souls. Mack was as aware of the historical setting in his first Olympics as anyone on Team USA. "I wanted to feel the spirit of the place," he said. Mack had studied Olympic history when he was getting his master's degree from the University of Tennessee. He brought a disciplined, almost severe appreciation of time and place with him to Athens. He always brought the same respect to Bubka's meet in Donetsk and to the Prefontaine Classic.

"Greece was the birthplace of the Olympics, so obviously it's a very important place to every track and field athlete," he said.

When the family gathered in the Mack home for Christmas in 2003, his mother Arlene presented everyone with a cap that read "Athens 2004." Mack also received a license plate frame with the logo on it. He stuck with the "Go Browns" frame he already had and never wore the cap. "It wasn't that I thought I would jinx myself," he said. "But I had too much respect for the place to tarnish it in any way. I did have the email address, Goldnathens, but that was a quiet confidence."

During qualifying, he knew he had violated his own rules of restraint. It is the Tim Mack version of the ancient Greeks' belief in self-control. "I got too into the surroundings, and it backfired on me," said Mack. "Every pole-vaulter likes to feel the energy of the crowd, but you can feed off the fans only to a point. It was so loud and so crazy and went on so long that I got too pumped up. It was more than I could handle."

There has always been a dichotomy in Greek life. The ancient Greek believed his own body was a battleground in which the sun god Apollo's reason vied for the upper hand with the wine god Dionysus' passion. On the holiest shrine in ancient Greece at Delphi, words attributed to the legendary lawgiver Solon were carved into the rock: "Nothing in excess."

But how couldn't you go overboard in your first Olympics, particularly in Greece, where it all began? The first thing Mack had done after getting home from the Trials was go to Wal-Mart and buy a $500 video recorder. It was with him every step of the way in the Opening Ceremonies. It was used in his brief photo op with LeBron James.

"There was no way I wasn't going to be at Opening Ceremonies," he said. "But it was six hours on your feet, too. It went so fast when you finally marched out that you almost couldn't enjoy it. Afterward, Toby and I sat with our lower legs in buckets of ice at the USOC training center. We figured we might as well get a head start toward recovery."

Mack would keep his focus at all costs. Russ Johnson had sent him a video that was almost eerily accurate in predicting the future. It ended with a digital photo Johnson had made with a little computer magic, one that showed Mack holding his arm high with a gold medal draped around it. "I dubbed in my voice like the P.A. man," Johnson said. "'Please turn your attention to the pole vault pit where Tim Mack has just won the gold medal and set an Olympic record.' It was so weird. It went exactly that way, too."

Mack knew that watching motivational tape was like being inside the stadium for Fani Halkia's victory lap. He couldn't view it often. "My nervous system would have been shot if I did," Mack said. "I always tried to be like Bubka before a competition. He said he was always calm before a major meet. I tried to be introverted, too."

In his notebook, Mack had written: "Conserve and excite." It was meet strategy. Conserve your energy; ignore extraneous activities. Then, when it's close to your turn, open yourself up to the energy of the surroundings and let yourself become excited. Such an approach required balance. Then again, if pole-vaulters don't know about keeping their bearings in strange surroundings, outside the comfort zone, who would?

Even Bragg—the Peter Pan of vaulting, whose antics seemed to typify the motto "I won't grow up"—was cautious at the Olympics. He would see John Thomas, the heavily favored American high jumper, dancing the night away in Rome in the Athletes' Village in 1960 and wonder if Thomas realized what was at stake. Sure enough, two Soviet jumpers finished ahead of the lanky American jumper. Thomas had left his legs on the dance floor.

"We got a feel for the Games, but just walking around and soaking it in wasn't for us. We had a goal, a mission. If we missed anything, it was well worth it," said Bemiller.

"I roomed with Derek Miles," Mack said. "That was fine, but I didn't want to make it too social. I got away for thirty minutes to an hour each day. You're there for a reason. You're there to win a gold medal."

It was a thin line Bemiller and Mack were walking. At least they knew where to get the shoes.

Mack went to Europe after the Trials supremely confident. Ever since the Prefontaine, he had known little but victory. But many things can suddenly go wrong in pole vaulting. Few of them are more wrong than showing up with a smile on your face, a song in your heart and no poles. Every pole-vaulter has such lost luggage stories, although how such ungainly bundles get overlooked or misplaced by baggage handlers is a mystery to them all.

Mack arrived in France for the Paris grand prix meet with no poles. "They assured me they would be there when I checked in," he said. "It has happened before. It will happen again." He borrowed the poles of Russia's Igor Pavlov. But every pole-vaulter has his own procedure with his own poles. With strange poles, Mack didn't trust the notebook, and he no-heighted. "I wasn't mentally into it," he said. "Rather than trust the numbers, I thought an easier way was to make the softer poles work. I was really pissed afterward."

Averbukh won at 18–10¼.

Hartwig, so bitterly disappointed in Sacramento, his own chance at the gold long gone, offered Mack encouragement. "There will be plenty of other meets for you," Hartwig said.

When the poles arrived at last before the next competition in Stockholm, Mack was a meet behind in devising the proper adaptations. "Stockholm was really my first meet in Europe, and I was still making adjustments from the last competition," said Mack, who finished third there with a vault of 18–6½ (5.65). Denis Yurchenko from Ukraine won at 5.71 (18–8¾.)

Mack wouldn't vault below 19 feet the rest of the summer. He won his last seven meets and 10 of his last 11. "Going into Athens, I was almost on autopilot," Mack said. "I was walking around, so confident, so comfortable, nobody had anything on me. I could feel it. These guys aren't even going to know what hit them. I was in the zone. Even if my jumps weren't good, I was clearing bars."

He won the Heusden Grand Prix in Brussels at 19–0¼ (5.80). At the prestigious Weltclasse meet in Zurich, a prime indicator of Olympic performance, he jumped 19–2¼ (5.85) and won. "Eighteen-eight had been my best in Zurich until then," said Mack.

Zurich is the best event of the European season annually, but Mack put even more importance on it. "I treated it as the Olympic final," he said. "I knew the same people were going to be in Athens, and I wanted to use it as my final tune-up, because I wasn't going to be jumping for more than two weeks."

Mack spent an idyllic two weeks of training in Crete, where Bemiller joined him. Both Mack and Grace Upshaw, who had qualified for the Olympic long jump in Sacramento, developed such a taste for the island's olive oil that they would order more bottles after returning to the States. "The whole island was Paradise," said Mack.

On their last night together on Crete, Mack bought a bottle of red Greek wine and tucked it into his backpack along with plastic water glasses from his room. He called Upshaw and suggested they take a walk. It was ten o'clock at night, with the moonlight a gold ribbon on the Mediterranean Sea, when Mack opened the wine. "I always wanted to drink wine on a beach," he said to her.

"I was shocked but pleasantly shocked," said Upshaw. "It was the first time he had ever made a gesture like that. And it was such a romantic gesture."

Their romance remained a secret, so it didn't capture the headlines, as did American hammer thrower Harold Connolly's courtship of Czechoslovakia's Olga Fikotova, his future wife, in the 1956 Olympics. Mack and Upshaw had, however, first met in track-appropriate circumstances. "It was the National Indoors that Tim won [in 2002] in New York. We were sitting next to each other, waiting for our drug tests," Upshaw said.

As Team USA headed to Greece, Mack took a hard-eyed look at his competition.

"Everybody goes there to win the gold medal," he said. "Some will fall short. Some didn't have a chance to start with. There have been a lot of meets where I went in thinking of winning, and I had no right to think that because I wasn't jumping high enough. I don't know if anybody loses the gold, because nobody is guaranteed it. A handful of guys have a chance to win it. But I think Toby and I both knew it would come down to us two. Nobody else was jumping like we were."

Just as pole vaulting requires strength and suppleness, just as it is contested on the ground and in the air, so Mack was a blend of opposites: practicality and idealism. He had thought out the sport as fully as anyone since Bubka. He had revamped his body. He was, as the dreamer Don Quixote and the sensible Sancho Panza were in combination, a reasonable idealist.

Track and Field News, the self-styled "Bible of the Sport," in its print preview of the Olympics, picked Stevenson to win, with Averbukh second, and Italy's Guiseppe Gibilisco third. "I don't think they knew Gibilisco had been injured and had only trained fifteen days before the Olympics," said Mack. "I didn't look closely at the rankings. It would just be extra energy. I'd be thinking, 'I can't believe they didn't pick me.'"

If the "Bible of the Sport" hadn't read "The Book" of Mack, it still noticed his superb form coming to Athens. In a later preview that was sent to subscribers by e-mail during the Olympics, *Track and Field News* picked Mack to win. Meanwhile, *Sports Illustrated* picked Stevenson to finish first and Mack to win the bronze medal. "Both magazines should have picked Toby," said Mack. "He had the best jump in the world to that point. He had cleared six meters. But I said to myself, 'They don't know me.'"

Bemiller liked his pupil's chances as well. "He was ready in his confidence. He got a late boost in confidence between the Prefontaine and the Trials. Everybody was jumping 18–8 to 19–0. Only three guys had made 19–2¼—Tim, Toby and Averbukh."

Mack and Bemiller had made a minute study of Olympic Stadium. It had the same configuration as Hornet Stadium at Sacramento State, with the two pole vault runways on the crown at the end of the field.

"I had talked to the coach of Mike Tully, the 1984 silver medalist in the pole vault, who has done a lot of work on stride pattern," Bemiller said. "It was the same problem as Sacramento. You run uphill and then downhill. In the elite facilities in the United States—Tennessee, Oregon, Modesto—the pits are parallel to the straightaways, so you get less swirling wind and no crown.

"When you run the uphill part, you have to keep your posture. You also don't cover as much ground because it's uphill, so you move your marks up a little. When you start downhill, you turn it over [stride] faster, and you cover ground faster."

Sacramento had been a cloud-seeding circus, a jumper's delight. As a pole-vault coach, however, Bemiller has seen better venues. "We just got lucky and had a good day with the conditions in Sacramento," he said.

"B" did like the steeper pitch to the stands of the much larger Olympic Stadium. It would act as a windscreen. Also, the competition would be held in the evening. Usually, the wind died down in Athens at nightfall. This meant all of Mack's painstakingly calculated figures, based on the wind being dead, would probably hold.

A final complication would present itself the night of the final. To speed the process along, two runways and two pits were set up in qualifying. Mack had vaulted on a different runway than in the final. "It made the start point a little different, and that concerned me," he said.

Mack was the oldest pole-vaulter in the Top Ten in the world rankings. Eight years had built to one moment. He had stayed with it and stayed with it and stayed with it until he became Calvin Coolidge's kind of guy. He had stayed with it through defeat, disappointment, and near despair, through injury, through penury, stayed with it when everything, including common sense, said he should cut his losses. Now, Mack was about to apply all the lessons so painfully learned. The dark horse was about to come from behind. The thatcher's son was going jousting.

The frenzy of competition began with the stillness of belief. On the morning of August 27, the day of the Olympic pole vault final, eight members of the Mack clan went to St. Nicholas Greek Orthodox church in the Plaka. When they left, eight candles they had lighted for Mack burned in a sand bucket.

Tim's cousin Gary Laco rollerbladed to the top of Lykabettos hill, which looks down on the Acropolis. Only hikers, extreme sports enthusiasts, or the very devout attend services at the wedding-cake white church, St. Leviticus, on its summit. Laco, although not particularly religious, felt he was channeling the spiritual feelings that surrounded Tim. He also left a candle burning.

In suburban Buffalo, the white nuns, as they had also done two days earlier for qualifying, as they had done in Sacramento at the Trials, were murmuring the words to the rosary. They dedicated one decade of beads to Tim Mack.

In Canton, Ohio, Ralph Schreiber, Brian Kelly, and others who had known Mack had logged onto the Internet and were waiting for the symbols that determined over (o), miss (x), or pass (p) to appear on their screens during the pole vault final.

In Augusta, Georgia, Russ Johnson, finishing his training as a physical therapist, had returned from the hospital where he was working with geriatric patients who had undergone hip and knee replacements. His computer was warming up too.

In Cleveland, Chico Kyle was teaching class. Storms were possible in the afternoon, when he would hold football practice.

In Athens, Bemiller, wearing a white golf shirt—not a beach shirt—and a red cap to be easily visible, returned from the poet sandalmaker's shop in plenty of time to visit with a calm and relaxed Mack on the warm-up track. "B" claimed his seat in the front row of the Olympic Stadium, near the pole vault pit. He saved two seats for his friends and fellow vaulting coaches, Greg Hull and Ralph Lindemann. "I was right in front where Tim could see me easily," he said.

He had his pick of seats. It was 4 P.M. in Athens. He was four hours early.

At 6 P.M., Bemiller, who had been in constant contact with Mack by cell phone, got a rude stare from an Australian coach who had just made his way to the vaulting area. The Aussie's only job was to reserve seats for the Down Under contingent. Two hours ahead should have been plenty of time. "He was pissed," said Bemiller. "I was such a rookie; I didn't know when to get there."

Later, the whole "pole-vaulting crew," as Bemiller called them, would squeeze into seats around him. They were the top coaches in the world, the flight controllers of never-never land. "I had idolized those guys, and there I was, coaching against them," said Bemiller.

Tim O'Hare rose from his pallet on the floor of former University of Tennessee decathlete Grant Cleghorn's apartment on Marathonus Ave., named for the fishing village that was the site of both the battle of Marathon and the start of the twenty-six-mile, 285-yard race named after it. O'Hare got to his seat in plenty of time to see his best man vault.

The women's long jump final began at 8 P.M., five minutes after the men's pole vault. It would end at 9:45 P.M. Upshaw finished tenth and didn't qualify for the final three jumps. Mack admitted later that he occasionally peeked at the long jump standings and tried to watch her jumps.

When the women's 4X100 relay runners tore around the third turn, near the pole vault pit, Stevenson stopped to watch. "Where are we? Aren't we in this?" he wondered, not knowing that the Americans had been disqualified for an illegal pass of the baton.

"Was that going on at the same time?" Mack said when asked about it later. "I honestly didn't even know that event was taking place."

In the jumping order for the final, Mack jumped third and Stevenson fourth. The two top guns would fire back to back like duelists.

During the long, tense night, Mack found that the visualization techniques begun in 2000 with Joe Whitney made him feel right at home. He basked in the glow of the Olympic flame because had warmed himself with it countless times in his mind. He had jumped toward the cauldron many times in his imagination.

"When I walked onto that field, I was thinking, 'which way is the wind blowing?'" Mack said. "I was thinking I had to warm up. Nothing else came into play. It was my coach and me. The crowd was there for energy, but nobody else existed. It's over time that you come to master that."

The imagination, Mack would prove, is an attribute, as much as speed or strength.

"Tim's event was even more difficult because it came near the end of the Olympics," Whitney said. "It's easy to get caught up in the emotion and the excitement of what's been happening. With everything that was going on in the pole vault, with his relationship with Grace Upshaw, with this being his first Olympics, it was really remarkable that he was able to stay in the moment." Bemiller's script for the final was as prescient as Johnson's digitally doctored photo.

The coach had much to consider: the time between attempts, the demands of jumping again after only one day's rest, the time between jumps as related to the size of the field, and the likely increments of the competitive progression. "B" knew that in seven of the ten Olympiads since the real advent of the fiberglass pole in 1964 the winning pole-vaulter had set an Olympic record. The old mark was 5.92 (19–5), set in Atlanta in 1996. "I put a check mark by 5.95 [19–6¼]. I thought that would win," Bemiller said. "I didn't want Tim to back in or win because nobody jumped high. I wanted to go out there against the best in the world, and I wanted him to jump well."

"We planned not to jump at 19 feet," added Bemiller, eliminating the fractions. "We were going to jump at 19–2, then every bar after that."

The sixteen-man final was the largest since twenty qualified in Montreal in 1976. It caused Mack to make a small adjustment in his preparations. "Knowing it was going to be a long competition, I ate a little more than I should have," said Mack. "I had three small meals. I felt a little full, but I was okay once I got over the first two bars."

Three jumpers went out at 18–6½, including Lobinger. Mack, still ruing the extra meal, had his first glitch at the height, needing a second try to clear. It would almost cost him the gold medal. Typical of the way this particular knight's visor admitted a glimpse only of shiny possibilities, he remained upbeat even after the miss. "When Lobinger went out, I felt the waters were parting," said Mack.

On the same bar, Pavel Gerasimov of Russia, who had jumped 18–11 (5.77), missed the pit. It was one more reminder, at the highest level in the world, the Olympic final, that the danger of the descent is as much a part of pole vaulting as the rise to the gabled roofs of possibility. Gerasimov took off far to the right side, clipped the bar off, and sliced over the right standard like a missed extra point in football. He landed flat on his back on the infield, unmoving. The crowd seemed to flinch as one, and a low moan—"Ohhhhhh!"—keened through the stadium.

"I saw him out of the corner of my eye, and I knew he wasn't going to make the pit. I thought, 'God, he doesn't know,'" Mack said.

Said Bubka: "He [Gerasimov] was too far right when he planted, and he tried to save the attempt. You must remember: you are a human being, not a machine."

Medical personnel rushed to Gerasimov, who lay sprawled on his back. For ordinary people, it would be IVs and "get the stretcher" at this point. Pole-vaulters are different. Eventually, the Russian got to his feet, rubbing his lower back. He passed until 18–10¼ (5.75), but halted his run halfway to the box because the pain was too much. He then withdrew.

"To be a pole-vaulter," as Gibilisco said, "you have to be a little bit crazy."

"I couldn't believe he was walking around and tried to jump," Mack said. "This sounds bad, but you can't be worrying about someone else. My thought was that they had medical staff to take care of him. In the pole vault, you should expect everything, anything, and nothing, as they say."

Five more men went out at 18–10½. The shocker was Averbukh, who bailed on his third attempt and rode his pole into the pit. "They were dropping like flies," said Mack. "I didn't know what to expect with Averbukh. Technically, he was wound tight, really explosive. He is an 8,000-point decathlete, so he was damn legitimate."

Miles needed a third jump to clear the same bar. Ecker, another six-meter man, would reach a season best by clearing on his first try.

By 19–0¼, every jump might mean a medal. Stevenson, who had gotten the crowd into it after an early clearance with a belly dancer's "shimmy-shake" of his hands and hips, had a clean record, but so did Gibilisco.

The daredevils scratched their heads and pondered what to do next. With Mack, there was never a question. "They were all scrambling, trying to figure out who was going to pass. Toby asked Tim if he was passing," said Bemiller. Mack never hesitated. "They only give medals to three guys, so a jump there might have been in the money," said Bemiller. "A little doubt crept in with me."

Mack walked toward Bemiller, who hid the doubt behind the generic question: "How ya feelin'?"

"No way I am jumping this height," said Mack.

Mack is a man who sticks with the process. His coach approved the decision and thought it meant Mack's eyes were on the ultimate prize. "See, if you're just thinking of the top three, you're not thinking of winning," said Bemiller.

Five men passed in all at 19 feet. Two of the passes were by Miles, after a first-attempt miss, and by Lars Borgeling of Germany, who had two misses. Igor Pavlov then cleared to take the lead. It was a career best for the Russian. But his lead lasted only long enough for Gibilisco to leave the bar quivering on the pegs at 19–2¼ (5.85). The surprise World Champion in 2003 at Paris, when he cleared 19–4¼, Gibilisco had seemed too wounded to contend. But his coach was none other than Vitaly Petrov, Bubka's old coach.

"I could see some of the effects of Bubka's old coach," said Mack. "I could see similarities to Bubka in the way he carried himself and, technically, in the way he carried the pole, planted and finished his jumps. He was very active and explosive."

Gibilisco's clearance had followed earlier misses by Mack and Stevenson at 19–2¼. But the Italian was far from pulling off another surprise championship. "That bar is not going to be high enough today," Mack thought.

Mack uncorked his best jump of the Olympics to clear easily. Now at least the silver medal would go to him if no one jumped higher. But Stevenson, next on the runway, went up, up and away, too.

Miles with the two chances he had left couldn't make the bar. Borgeling failed with his one try. Miles would finish seventh, Borgeling sixth. Ecker, done at 19–0¼, would be fifth.

Four were left—Gibilisco, the leader with a clean record, Stevenson, Mack and Pavlov, who passed his third at 19–2¼.

On his next jump, Mack matched his PB from the Trials at 19–4¼.

But Stevenson had plugged into the clapping, pleading, encouraging energy from the stands as well. He put a big jump of his own on top of Mack's. When Stevenson popped to his feet in the pit, the Toby Stevenson jump fest and 40 Licks tour had come rockin' into Athens. He raked at an unseen guitar's invisible strings with his hand, playing, perhaps, a silent version of "Satisfaction."

"I knew I had a medal, I just didn't know which one," Stevenson said. "I figured 5.90 would medal. Tim and I were back to back all day, which made it more exciting. He threw it in my face, and then I came right back."

Gibilisco stared at the bar he had cleared for his World Championship, as if visualizing a repeat performance. He ran to the box, planted, swung up toward the dark sky, and then aborted, sailing under the bar. He then passed, saving two tries for 19–6¼ (5.95). He would make no good attempt at that height either, finishing with the bronze medal.

Pavlov, on the periphery of the drama, finished fourth after his miss at 5.95.

It had come down to Mack and Stevenson, as both had known it would.

Track and field is at its best when it features head-to-head matchups. Carl Lewis vs. Ben Johnson in the Olympic 100-meter final had the aura of a heavyweight title fight. The hybrid 150-meter race between Donovan Bailey and Michael Johnson after the Atlanta Olympics briefly took track beyond its usual status as a niche sport. Heike Drechsler vs. Jackie Joyner-Kersee in the women's long jump and Renaldo Nehemiah vs. Greg Foster in the 110 hurdles were rivalries of all-time greats.

Mack vs. Stevenson was a purist's rivalry, free of the vanity and arrogance that often mars the sprints. Their duel broadened the appeal of the pole vault by pitting opposites—introversion and "let's party" exuberance—against each other in a sky fight over the most coveted prize in sports: an Olympic gold medal.

Only Stevenson, jumping on the longest pole of anyone (17–0½) and holding at the very top of it to Mack's slightly lower grip on a 16–8¾ pole, had been to the outer limits of six meters. Stevenson had the past success; Mack had the new horizon. He had experience; Mack had momentum. He had the name; Mack had "The Book." And in it, Tim Mack would soon write an Olympic record.

Both Mack and Stevenson missed their first two jumps. Stevenson ran through the pit on his first try. This was a more serious setback than simply dislodging the bar in the riptides and chop at the edge of big air. "I ran through the first time, and that was not conducive to coming back with a good chance," he said.

Both Tim and "B" were surprised Stevenson didn't fight the vault through to its conclusion. Each attempt is a chance to learn on the pole's curve. Failure to launch takes that away. Mack had spent years gaining the knowledge of how to control his body and where to plant which pole with the standards at what setting in order to jump as big as his dreams.

"You can't wait on the jump," Bemiller said. "Unless you are in an unsafe position, you always attack all the way through the jump. If you don't, you don't know what adjustments to make, so your second jump is really your first."

After Mack's second miss O'Hare caught Bemiller's eye. Knowing that Stevenson was leading on fewer misses, O'Hare shouted to Bemiller: "Way to go! Silver!" Bemiller glared back. "He didn't want to hear it," said O'Hare.

"I had to believe, so Tim could believe too," Bemiller said.

The difference between first and second now was one miss, Mack's failed try way back at 18–6½. Bemiller pulled out the yellow index cards on which he kept the same data as in Mack's notebook, checking to make sure the pole was right for the height and the standards were at the proper spot for the jump.

Petrov snorted in derision. "You should have that in your head," the Russian said.

Assured that he and his coach were on the same index card, Mack walked to the runway for his third try at a bar no one had ever cleared in the Olympics. It was his tenth jump of the Olympic final. The event takes so much out of jumpers that most pole-vaulters are at their best over no more than a half-dozen attempts. But Mack had stuck with it. Now he faced the moment that would prove Calvin Coolidge correct.

"You are not going to lose. You have worked for this moment too long," he said, in a murmured pep talk.

"Goldnathens went through my head," he said. "I set that up and I didn't call it Silvernathens."

Mack moved his starting point back one foot, to 135 feet, 6 inches. He knew the adrenaline pump would be wide open. "That was a part of it," said Bemiller. "You're so pumped. But do you trust yourself to move back a little bit because of it?"

Mack had chosen a stiffer pole, and he propped it on his shoulder and raised his arms above his head, slamming his palms together, rhythmically clapping, as the late-night crowd caught the beat. It was contagious. The whole stadium began clapping along with him. The Athenians were more enthusiastically into audience participation than people dressed in funny costumes ever were on *Let's Make a Deal!* They had repeatedly done "The Wave," leaping in unison from their seats and raising their arms.

From somewhere high above Mack, Gary Laco's whistle shrieked in the tumult. Mack could hear him, knew it was their recognition signal, but he couldn't find him. In the stands, O'Hare had been jumping to his feet as soon as Mack was on the runway, gauging when the wind was just right, waiting to give the "go" signal to his best man, the man who had coached him, the "man for others" whom the Jesuits had taught well.

"Down in front! Down in front!" the Greek spectators shouted.

"They were cheering, 'Hellas! Hellas!' pretty loud when any of their athletes was doing something," said O'Hare, resentfully. "But the Greek guy next to me and Grant Cleghorn was happy. It was obvious we knew one of the guys competing, so he was cheering with us."

When O'Hare gave him the signal, Mack brought his arms down and the pole up. It was late night, the lights that reminded him of Friday nights in high school were on, and his whole career was about to be defined in the world's brightest spotlight.

"He will make this," Don Mack said, simply, to Arlene. "He has worked too hard for this not to. He has poured his heart and soul into it."

Every other event was over but the pole vault. The jumpers had been out there for nearly three and a half hours, but that was still only an eye blink compared to the old days when a pole-vaulter seemed to start a meet as a boy and end as Tarzan by the meet's conclusion.

"If you start thinking about a personal best or an Olympic record, you put too much pressure on yourself. I couldn't focus on losing it all in a split-second," Mack said. "I wasn't jumping to win at that point, just to stay alive. So I was just thinking about two technical things. I was thinking about posture and arms. It was taking everything you believe and trust to do this."

As the thunder from the stands amped his adrenaline even more, Mack muttered his vaulting keys.

"Work your arms!"

"Keep your posture!"

"You will make this!"

It was three years after he started Goldnathens, four years after the last Olympic opportunity, eight years after he started reaching Olympic Trials, and almost nineteen years after he started pole vaulting.

Nothing else is close to Olympic sports for putting so much of an athlete's competitive life on the line. Nothing else asks such a commitment of the Churchillian qualities of blood, sweat, toil and tears, or reveals so much of a man's innermost dreams to the world. In Tim Mack, the man had met the moment, and he would make it his own.

At 11:24 P.M. in Athens, Mack began his run, headed for the stars.

"B" never thought it was a good idea to bombard his pole-vaulters with too many specifics during a meet. "I don't want them to hit a mark. If they get in rhythm and start running better, the takeoff would come out okay," he said.

On good days, Mack launched at 13½ feet. Usually, he was more like 13–2 to 13–5.

Hartwig launched farther out, and so do many of the Euros. But it is all a balancing act. "You can be gripping high and taking off from far out, and it still might not translate into height because your swing is not effective," Bemiller said.

Mack ran heaven-bound and hell-bent. Even with the deeper start, he covered the ground in huge gulps. "I overran," said Mack, "which I was afraid of doing."

He was "under" on his takeoff, taking off a stride too close to the box. It was Sacramento all over again.

"On his best jumps, he's clean on the takeoff, and the pole moves faster. Instead, he got jammed," said Bemiller.

Mack went up, bending the pole with the weight of his dreams, cracking the code of the air by staying with the jump when it seemed lost. As the pole's recoil lashed him upward, he knew he was in trouble.

"Halfway through, I thought I was going to miss it," he said. "I thought I was going to hit the bar on the ascent."

That was how it all came to grief at Sacramento in the 2000 Trials. But that was then. This was now.

"He had to fight from the bottom up. Again," Bemiller said.

"It would have been real easy to abort. But on your last try, as close as you are to your dream, as close as you can possibly be, almost touching it—you can't abort," Mack said.

When Bemiller speaks about the 19–6 vault, it isn't in biomechanical terms. It's in the tones of Knute Rockne whipping the Fighting Irish into a froth with a fiery pep talk.

"Hit with your hands. Attack," Bemiller said.

The numbers in his book had taken away doubt and now would redefine the Olympic record.

The prayers in Lackawanna, New York, the soft candlelight in St. Nicholas and St. Leviticus, the karmic bank in which Mack had made so many deposits while working for others—none of that hurt.

The blisters on his hands from the work in Bemiller's yard, the teabags, the Dodge Omni, the pre-dawn bike rides to the rec center to clean toilets, the spurned sponsorship letters, the M&D Track Club, the hobbled year without the sport he loved so much, the three-year plan based on deprivation—all fueled his trip to the bar as well.

Maybe muscles have memory too. Maybe only someone who had devoted himself, mind and body, heart and soul, as completely as Mack to pole vaulting could synchronize the required moves in his sinews, independent of thought, apart from the suffocating pressure.

Mack twisted and got off the pole, and now it was ballet two stories off the ground. The Greek drama was at its peak as he writhed over the bar, his knees staying out of harm's way by a margin of—what? a votive candle's guttering flame?

He pumped his fists and screamed in triumph all the way down then sprang to his feet in the pit, still bellowing while the roar from the stands engulfed him.

In the stands, Tim O'Hare was cheering so hard that you would have thought the Vols were beating Florida and the band was belting out "Rocky Top." When another buddy, decathlete Chad Smith, came running over, a standing eight-count practically had to be issued. "When Tim wriggled over, I started throwing my arms around and going crazy, and I punched Chad in the nose by accident," O'Hare said.

His parents hugged in their seats and wept.

Upshaw had found a seat on the second level of the stadium. She went racing down the stairs to field level, screaming in glee.

In Canton, Ohio, Kelly and Schreiber were on the phone to each other, laughing and cheering. "Our computer screens were refreshing at different speeds, so we thought this way, if one of us found out the results first, he could tell the other," Mack's old coach said.

In Augusta, Georgia, Russ Johnson started hurrahing over the phone to his father. Look what had happened to the skinny kid who looked like he didn't belong in the Georgia Dome. "Oh, my God! He made it!" cried Johnson.

Standing near the pole vault runway, Toby Stevenson, in his heart of hearts, didn't think he was going to need another jump. As Mack came screaming out of the pit, Stevenson shook his head. He hadn't counted on that. He had expected the gold, not everything, anything and nothing.

"I was surprised he jumped 5.95," Stevenson said. "You don't think about somebody jumping a personal record and an Olympic record on his last attempt."

"Toby felt he was in control," said Bubka. "I think he thought he had already won. Timothy got a very strong belief in himself from the Trials. It was too early for Toby to think: 'This is enough.'"

Mack climbed out of the pit, angry that he had let go of as much as he had. "I was a little pissed at myself for celebrating that I had cleared," he said. "It's like golf. You tell yourself that the guy you are playing will make his putt. You don't take anything for granted. I told myself Toby would make it, and then, we would jump at six meters."

As Stevenson went to the runway, one thing Bubka, "The Master," had said stuck in his head like a photo in an album. Said Stevenson: "Bubka always said to clear it by a ton, then you can make adjustments."

"I didn't even watch," said Bemiller. "I couldn't. I could tell what happened from the crowd reaction."

Mack wasn't looking either. He was psyching up to jump six meters.

Stevenson cleared it by a ton. But he brushed the bar off on the way down. "That's the pole vault," he said.

Stevenson rose, howling in frustration, and spiked his helmet on the pads.

"I think my steps were a little under where I wanted to be," he said.

It is another of the opposites pole-vaulters must balance. They get "under" when they get overexcited. "Maybe if the standards were five centimeters [two inches] closer, I'd have made it," said Stevenson.

That, of course, was one of the final adjustments Bemiller and Mack had made after the Pre. They had moved the standards in, from the maximum depth of 80 centimeters to 50–60. Thirty centimeters is about a foot. For the narrower arc Mack got when he was "under" on the takeoff, it was the perfect adjustment.

In Cleveland, the storm that had been brewing all day had hit.

"We get these strange, sudden storms off Lake Erie," Chico Kyle said. "August is football season in Ohio. We were on the practice field, and I could see these terrible, crazy clouds forming. The wind changed, and they swept in off the lake."

Kyle thought he had about two minutes before the storm hit.

"Two minutes later, bang! We got hit," he said. "I ran around, gathering up the leather footballs. On a Catholic school budget, they can't be damaged in the rain. I ran into my office to get the composite cover balls."

Rory Fitzpatrick, the assistant athletic director, had been on the computer, too. "My God!" he cried. "Tim Mack just won the gold medal!"

"I would never have known it if the storm hadn't hit," Kyle said. "I think the Lord wanted me to run in there."

In one great leap upward, Mack, competing on a world stage against the best in his sport, had become the school's most illustrious athlete ever.

Mack had led only once, on the golden jump. He had four misses, the equal of the most ever by a gold medalist. Only twice since jump-by-jump records were first kept in the 1928 Olympics had anyone gone on to win the gold medal after so much struggle. His ten jumps to win equaled Richards in 1956 for the most ever. His thirteen jumps overall (counting three misses at six meters after the golden jump) are the most ever in an Olympic final.

It was a masterpiece of strategic thinking. "All night, I kept waiting for those guys, the best in the world, to step up. Only Toby and Tim did," Bemiller assessed.

"People do not realize what a great Olympic moment this was," said Whitney. "People seldom PR in the Olympic pole vault."

"People thought he was a dark horse, because he only jumped 13–6 in high school. But whatever he does, Tim Mack is a fierce competitor, whether it's golf, video games, or whatever," Russ Johnson said. "I knew deep inside he was going to win. It would not be right for him to finish second."

"He was the most deserving guy of any of them," O'Hare said.

In Athens, Bemiller was looking at Tim after he had become golden. "The fans wanted to celebrate," "B" said, "but Tim was going through his same routine."

"He's not through jumping yet," Bemiller thought.

"I don't want a hug or anything," Mack said, when he came over to talk to his coach.

Can you imagine any athlete—much less an athlete from America, where the vast popularity of *American Idol* demonstrates people's intense need to be a star—winning it all and not at least pausing to hold up an index finger, lest anyone think he was not the A-No.1, grain-waving, fruited-plain-treading ideal of athletic supremacy? Toby Stevenson would have danced all night.

"It showed how focused he was," said Bemiller. "He was going to go right at six meters. It would be easy to let up, because in your sub-conscious, you know it's been a long night—but not Tim. That's what sticks with me: He knew he was passing at 19 feet when all the others wondered what to do, and, after he won, everyone wanted to celebrate, and he wasn't done jumping."

Not even the gold medal was enough for the dark horse. The knight had won the tournament and gotten the girl, but his tale wasn't over. The gladiator had dropped his mask and revealed himself to be the general who had won the air war.

"When you look at it, when you realize even Bubka only won one Olympic gold medal, it makes you realize how incredible this was," Bemiller said. "Things might have been tough early in Tim's career, but he got one chance, and he made the most of it. Even the greatest in the world couldn't. The event beats you up, and add the politics, injuries, and everything else, and that he still came through, that's what makes it so special. It's magic, pure magic—this event and what Tim did."

As he talked with his parents after his third miss at six meters, officials told Mack to hurry up and take his victory lap already. It was after midnight in Greece, and Mack didn't even have time to put his spikes back on, so he ran it in his socks. As he turned to go, Cleghorn shoved a small Greek flag in his hand. Sometimes, Mack waved it. Sometimes, he let a large American flag stream behind him. He was Captain Midnight, running with the red, white and blue.

He wouldn't remember doing so, but he actually ran one and a half laps. It was fitting. It had been such a big victory.

The victory had never really been in the moment of 11:24 P.M., August 27. The victory was in all that went before that. The victory was created by everything Mack went through to get over that bar. He had provided the ultimate proof that it's never too late, that a man must keep trying and never give up.

He had given every plodder wings. For the air is where the glories of the world are—in autumn leaves flung like gold doubloons from a treasure chest, in a hawk riding a thermal air current, and in Tim Mack's summer of 2004.

Given how long he had waited, it was no surprise that he would have to wait a little longer before actually receiving his gold medal. The pole vault ended so late that the medal ceremony didn't take place until the next evening. Mack spent the night celebrating, including attending a victory party at his parents' hotel. There, he called together his parents and all his other relatives, as well as O'Hare and a couple of other members of the vaulting community.

"I couldn't have done it without you," Tim Mack said. "It wouldn't have meant as much if you weren't here."

He left at 6 A.M. to take a blood test for doping control. First, though, Mack stopped by the Athletes' Village where Upshaw was staying. "I only started to get to know her in May," he said. "My big regret is that she wasn't at the hotel. I had always been so focused, but now I had opened myself up a little more."

At the Athletes' Village, Mack text-messaged her. "U up?"

"Where r u?" she replied.

"Rite outside ur door," he said.

Grace tiptoed outside to meet him. Both are world-class athletes and were mindful of disturbing sleepers who might be competing that day.

"He was still in his track singlet he had worn when he won, still in his socks, and, frankly, smelling a little bit of alcohol," Upshaw said, laughing. "He had this great smile on his face, and I just jumped into his arms."

They sat on the hallway floor, whispering.

"You won!" she said.

"I know," he said.

"You're the gold medalist!" she said.

"I was just trying to win a meet," he said.

The whole, colossal quest for the grail was over, and Mack was still trying to grasp exactly how happy the ending was turning out to be.

"It's amazing," Mack said. "She is at the other end of the country, but we are making it work. I'm definitely not seeing her because it is convenient. It's challenging. Every day I am with her, I'm learning about myself."

"People say he is reserved," said Upshaw. "But I think he is the most affectionate person. He's always got his arm around me or touching me."

The medal ceremony the next night was overshadowed by the final game of the star-crossed USA men's Olympic basketball team, which defeated Lithuania for the bronze medal. By the time the ceremony started, Mack's parents had finally found seats in Olympic Stadium, which didn't necessarily mean they had found tickets.

"It was a real Keystone Cops comedy," Tim's mother said.

No one had thought to buy tickets for August 28, which was when the leftover medal ceremonies from the 27th would take place. Tim came up with four tickets, and "B" chipped in two, but the parents still didn't have tickets for themselves. In desperation, Don Mack bought a pair from a scalper minutes before the gates opened. He and Arlene walked through Olympic Park, past the swimming and diving stadium, past the gymnastics hall where the Not-Quite-Dream Team played. At the gate to the track stadium, a ticket taker shook her head. Don Mack peered closely at what he had bought for the first time.

"They were for the platform diving finals!" Arlene Mack said.

"I was so glad I could buy tickets, I never even looked at them," Don said.

"I could have killed him," Arlene said.

Officials finally took pity on them and put the Macks in premium box seats for the medal ceremony.

Before Tim Mack emerged from the tunnel, he had a perfect view of the medal podium and the fans packed into their seats. "I guess it's real after all," he thought.

Athens had been the "Make-Nice" Olympics for the USA. Because of the war in Afghanistan and Iraq, American fans and athletes had curbed the jingoism. Red, white, and blue attire was rare in the stands. Athletes listened to USOC lectures, urging them not to be sore winners.

"It wasn't like wearing a military uniform in any sense," Mack said, "but you still have a different sense of who you are and of what country you are from when you have 'USA' across your chest. There are 300 million people in the United States, and you're representing all of them. All the time I was in Athens, I reflected on that. I walked with my head a little bit higher. But those feelings are tenfold more powerful when you walk out to get the gold medal."

In this setting, Tim Mack—controlled, shuttered, his emotions clenched tight, almost down to the roots of his self-shorn hair—walked out and almost busted loose bawling.

Standing on the tallest step of the podium, flanked by Stevenson and Gibilisco, Mack, who had already been presented with an olive wreath by an attendant, dipped his head so that the distinguished IOC member from Ukraine, Sergey Bubka, could place the gold medal around his neck. When he did so, it almost looked as if he was making a reverent bow.

A moment later, he bit down on the medal, jokingly. Yep. It was genuine. No counterfeits on the victory podium.

When the American flag went up the pole and "The Star-Spangled Banner" began to play, Mack's eyes blurred with tears. Twice, he choked down sobs with deep, ragged breaths.

The man in the iron mask let his guard down. The guy who broke everything down into its component parts, the figure filbert fiddling with his numbers—that guy got lost along the way, stunned by the enormity of what he had done.

"That was what got to me," he said. "I thought about the road, the whole, long road, starting years ago, which led to the medal ceremony. I thought about what my parents must be feeling. I had been up forty-eight straight hours, and maybe that was part of it. Everything kind of slowed down. I wanted to stay in that moment."

"I was zooming the video camera in on Tim's face," said O'Hare. "It was hard, because I had tears in my eyes. I turned around, and Grant had tears rolling down his cheeks."

"I never saw that side of Tim. I thought that shell of his was going to break," said Russ Johnson, watching at home on TV.

When the ceremony was over in Athens, Bubka approached Mack, seeking a commitment for his meet in Donetsk in 2005.

Mack had tried to emulate Bubka all his life, across the gulf of warring political ideologies and vast distances, connecting with him on the pure level of love of the sport. Now, in a way, Mack had become the man on the poster of his bedroom wall.

"When is the meet?" Mack asked.

"When would you like it to be?" Bubka said.

Afterword
HARRY "BUTCH" REYNOLDS

*A*bove and Beyond captures the passion and love track and field athletes have for their sport. When you read about the sacrifices Tim Mack made to clear that bar in Athens, you do not wonder how Americans have achieved so much in the Olympics, but you are amazed that they have accomplished so much on their own, without the full-time coaching and financial support athletes receive in other countries.

Pole-vaulters remind me of guys driving race cars at 200 miles per hour. That's their mentality. It takes a different breed of guy to go 20 feet into the air on a pole that can break and then fall down on his back.

Ever since the Dan and Dave commercials before Barcelona, fans have understood how difficult the pole vault is. It is the biggest weight a decathlete has to carry. They are scared to death of it.

Bill Livingston's book shows how Tim Mack not only overcame that bar, but also overcame a system that forced him to work at part-time jobs to support himself. He really did go "Above and Beyond."

Butch Reynolds of Akron Hoban High School won the Olympic silver medal in the 400 meters in 1988 and also was a member of the gold medal–winning 4x 400-meter relay team then. He held the world record in the event for 11 years. Formerly the speed coordinator for the Ohio State football team, Reynolds is a member of the Ohio State University Athletics Hall of Fame.

Glossary

APPROACH: The sprint to the vaulting box. Usually eighteen to twenty strides for an elite competitor.

AQ: Automatic Qualifying mark.

FLEX RATING: The pole manufacturer determines this rating by placing a standardized amount of stress (usually a fifty-pound weight) on the pole and measuring how much the weight displaces the center of the pole. Two poles may be of the same length, but one can be considerably stiffer than the other.

GRIP: How close to the end of the pole a pole-vaulter takes hold with his top hand. A higher grip means a higher parabola and potential for a higher clearance. A lower grip provides easier penetration into the pit.

HYPERFLEXION: Excessive bending, technically forcing the bones closer together at a joint. In pole vaulting, it is also used to mean cervical strain, which is caused by stretching the spinal cord when a pole-vaulter rolls on his neck or head.

INVERTING: The point in a pole-vaulter's jump where his or her body is completely upside down, legs overhead. As the pole begins to straighten, the pole-vaulter extends his body in an "I" position as close to the pole as possible. The hips are as high as possible, while the shoulders and head rotate under with the body in line vertically.

MARKS: Visual indicators on the runway that enable the pole-vaulter to plot the course of his approach. Marks can be tape or even spare shoes strategically placed. The marks are at the start, the midpoint, and the desired takeoff point.

OUT/UNDER (OR OVER/UNDER): If a pole-vaulter runs too fast and overshoots his takeoff point, he is said to be "under," or too close. This means he is taking off, for example, 12 feet from the box instead of 13. The reverse is true for being "out," or too far away from the desired takeoff spot directly beneath the pole-vaulter's extended top hand.

PARABOLA: The arc of the vault. In a sense, the parabola is like an upside-down "u."

PB/PR: A pole-vaulter's personal best or personal record.

PERIODIZATION: A training theory based on building strength by frequently adjusting the volume and intensity of workouts. Studies have shown that periodization prevents performance plateaus associated with over-repetitive training. The athletes in the studies didn't gain additional muscle mass over the control group, so the increased strength is thought to be related to the way the nervous system controls sinews.

PIT: The landing pads. Formally made of sand in the formative days and then sawdust, the pit is now composed of foam rubber.

PLANT: The transfer of the pole into the slanted box. It is the most difficult aspect of the vault, running at full speed while using the hands to position the pole in an extended position overhead and preparing to take off.

PLYOMETRICS: Exercises stimulating the reactive properties of muscles, specifically, their ability to respond to different degrees of flexing or contracting. Plyometric training strengthens the leg and arm muscles necessary for the jumps and allows them to respond faster and more powerfully at the moment of takeoff.

POLE DROP: This is the term used to describe the process where the pole-vaulter lowers the pole gradually throughout the approach run while preparing for the plant. The pole-vaulter lowers the tip of the pole during the approach after starting out holding the pole in an almost vertical position at the beginning of the approach.

POLES: Originally solid hickory and ash, then the more pliable bamboo, steel, and now made of fiberglass and carbon/glass composites, these are the implements pole-vaulters use to touch the sky. Even a nick from a spike mark can create a fatal flaw in a pole. For world-class pole-vaulters, they cost about $500 each. Poles are also known as "sticks" in the pole vault community.

PULL-UP: When the pole is almost straight, the pole-vaulter pulls with both hands as his hips and center of gravity reach the height of the crossbar.

RELEASE: After doing what amounts to a handstand on the pole, the pole-vaulter's right hand releases the pole.

SOFTNESS: Usually a pole-vaulter uses the softest (easiest to flex) pole in qualifying because heights are lower.

STANDARDS: The uprights that hold the crossbar on pegs. They can be adjusted within the rules either closer to or farther from the box, depending on the depth of the pole-vaulter's jump and the conditions. Originally, they could be set from 30 to 80 centimeters (12 inches to about 32 inches) from the pit. Now, the NCAA forbids settings closer than 45 cm to avoid falls into the box.

STIFFNESS: A stiffer pole requires more speed and better technique to bend it, but can deliver more "kick" as it straightens. Pole-vaulters use stiffer poles when facing a higher bar.

SWING UP/ROCK BACK: After the execution of an aggressive takeoff, the pole-vaulter's takeoff leg (the "trail leg") will be fully extended. The vaulter then executes a violent whipping action that is similar to a gymnast performing a giant swing on the high bar. After this swing up, the athlete slightly tucks his or her knees as the trail leg catches the lead leg, increasing the speed of the rotation.

TAKEOFF: Pole-vaulters leap into the jump. In the optimal takeoff, the athlete's extended top hand should be over his takeoff foot. It has been described as "riding in a speeding convertible and jumping up to grab the bridge overpass above."

TAPPING: This is a warm-up and practice technique where a coach or fellow competitor gives a boost to a pole-vaulter. Usually, it consists of a slight push on the back at takeoff to increase confidence and momentum. Now, tapping is outlawed everywhere because of un-reasonable overuse leading to false confidence with pole-vaulters clearing heights only because of taps.

TURN/ROTATE: Almost simultaneously with the release, the pole-vaulter makes a half-turn counter-clockwise into the straightening pole. This move presents the pole-vaulter's chest to the crossbar.

VAULT BOX: The steel box that is embedded in the runway for the pole-vaulter to thrust the pole down into just prior to takeoff. Ideally padded on the collar and sides for safety, the vault box is slanted on the sides and back to allow the pole to bend and roll.

VOLZING: A now illegal practice named for pole-vaulter Dave Volz, who steadied the crossbar on its pegs with his hand as he went over. The pegs have been shortened from 3 inches to 2¼ inches, so any attempt at Volzing is just as liable to knock the bar off as keep it on.

WIND: A tailwind is the pole-vaulter's best friend, generating more speed in his approach. A crosswind requires varying tactical adjustments. A headwind (in his face) is the worst-case scenario. In essence, the vaulter/pole system constitutes a human sail. Dead calm is second-best.

WORKING THE ARMS: A violent, sweeping shoulder rotation, crucial to the pole-vaulter's ability to continue swinging on the straightening pole. Some analysts say it accounts for over one-third of the transition of energy to the pole from the run.